HAPPILY
EVER AFTER

Edward H. Scissons, Ph.D.

HAPPILY EVER AFTER

Making the Most of Your Retirement

DEMBNER BOOKS • NEW YORK

Dembner Books
Published by Red Dembner Enterprises Corp., 80 Eighth Avenue, New York, N.Y. 10011
Distributed by W. W. Norton & Company, Inc., 500 Fifth Avenue, New York, N.Y. 10110

Library of Congress Cataloging-in-Publication Data

Scissons, Edward H.
    Happily ever after.

    Includes index.
    1. Retirement—United States—Planning.   I. Title.
HQ1062.S38   1987   646.7'9   87-14346
ISBN 0-934878-92-7

To the memory of May Kathleen Scissons,
who would not be surprised

Contents

Acknowledgments

This book could not have been written without the continued support of the University of Saskatchewan and the willingness of Red Dembner to believe in new ideas.

Special thanks are due to Lorraine Blashill for reviewing the original manuscript and to Anna Dembner for her editing wisdom.

Finally, a note of recognition to Michael, who wanted to be read to when I wanted to write, Patrick, whose imagination in spending anticipated royalties knows no bounds, and Karen, who is ever so much better at practicing what I preach.

Retirement
and Change

"An unhatched egg is to me the greatest challenge in life."
—E. B. White, in a letter to Reginald Allen

Derek, aged sixty-seven, had been retired for three years from his position as chief process engineer with a midwestern plastics production plant. As a result of corporate cost-cutting he had been offered retirement one year in advance of his normal date and had snapped up the opportunity. His last two years with the firm had, by his own assessment, been unremarkable and he was glad to be "free."

After nine months of retirement Derek showed many of the signs of clinical depression. Nothing seemed to interest him any more. He had traveled very little during his working life and he and his wife had planned to travel extensively after retirement. They had done some traveling during the first months of his retirement but now his wife had to push to get him to take even short weekend trips. As well, the woodworking hobby he pursued enthusiastically for forty years no longer interested him and he talked of selling his once-prized tools.

Derek's wife was beside herself. "All our life we did without things so we would have a good retirement. Now we've got money, time, and good health and yet he sits there like a bump on a log. We had more fun when he was working."

There is a crisis in our nation today. It is a crisis that has been building since the late 1940s and one that can only get worse. You do not see it highlighted on the evening news and its victims seldom complain. It is there nonetheless. That crisis is retirement and it is measured in waste—waste of the human spirit.

In our typical way we have dealt with the symptoms of this crisis. Retirement, we are told, should be financially secure and for middle-income people we have made it financially secure. Retirement should be healthy and for the bulk of middle-income earners we have made it healthy. But retirement, like the life that comes before it, should be meaningful and many retirees fail miserably to make it so.

For working people the key words today are fulfillment and excellence, the joy of doing well at that which you enjoy. It is ironic that the very attributes encouraged in the workplace—attributes that foster self-esteem—are often denied once paid work is concluded. In fact, our society often goes one step further by equating retirement with anticipated freedom—freedom to do nothing. At its worst, the prisoner and the retiree share a common fate. Both are free only if freedom is the absence of required meaningful activity.

Retirement must be more than *leaving something behind*. To retire is not simply to leave your work behind and do nothing. That is a sure-fire recipe for depression. A real retirement is moving on, moving on to a new agenda, an agenda that offers you something more than the absence of work. For work, no matter how inconsequential you think it is now, is important to you although you may not recognize this importance until you retire.

Retirement must be a "going to," not simply a "going away from."

It was hard to think of Alice as retired. At seventy she was often mistaken for "fifty-five and holding," her eyes yielding a sparkle that would put many teenagers to shame. Retired from her high-school teaching position for ten years, Alice seemed busier now than many of her younger friends. When there was an interesting project on the go, chances are that you would find Alice involved "up to her eyeballs."

"I knew that I would need something to keep me going once I

retired," she confided. "I was always so busy with the kids: teaching, band coordination, and school sports. You can't just pull the plug on those kinds of things once you retire or you might as well pull the plug on yourself."

Over the ten-year period since her retirement Alice had chaired a regional teachers advisory committee, started an international travel club for retired teachers, worked as a volunteer for more than fifteen community associations, completed three university courses in noneducation topics, and written a score of articles in the pop-education press. Many of her activities still involved students—"It's the cheapest way I know to keep yourself young," she said, laughing.

As in any crisis, there are those who steer through retirement unscathed. There are those who are successful not because they do not have the same problems and shortcomings as the rest of us, but because they have overcome these problems, turned adversity into opportunity. Such individuals are to retirement what Tom "In Search of Excellence" Peters' *champions* are to business—winners who consistently flow against the tide of mediocrity. This book is about such champions.

Retirement Today

Worrying about impending retirement is a lot like worrying about good health—a luxury many of us wish we could afford! In a historical perspective, both types of worry are pretty recent. A hundred years ago planned retirement was rare, and if you did retire, you were unlikely to live long enough to worry about it. With the ever increasing likelihood of survival past seventy and with the seventy-five-plus age group the fastest growing age segment in our nation, retirement is a luxury that most of us are going to have to afford, like it or not.

Surviving retirement involves two major dimensions, the material and the psychological. As a society and as individuals, we have dealt adequately with the first and largely ignored the second. Pension plans, retirement savings plans, annuities, long-term investments and even something as simple as compound-interest savings accounts have removed much of the economic fear of retirement for middle-income North America. As well, we are healthier and have an enviable medical system to keep us that way longer. Even with modest means, the average middle-income individual can look forward to, if not a sumptuous retirement, then at least one that will be both financially adequate and long standing.

The other side of retirement, the psychological side, centers on change, change not only in what you will do with your life but, more importantly, in who you are. How you react and adapt to these changes will dictate how successful you will be in your retirement. It is possible to enjoy your retirement but that enjoyment will not just "happen"—it must be pursued as actively as you have pursued any desirable job in the preretirement phase of your life.

Good retirements do not just happen—they are built.

People used to joke that Robert had been planning his retirement for more years than he had been working. Now sixty-one, retired for three years on an accelerated program from his civil service administrative position, Robert was a picture of retirement bliss. During his last five years of paid work he had become heavily involved with the international student exchange program of his local Rotary club and carried this avocation into his retirement with real enthusiasm.

In the past three years, during which he had suffered a minor heart attack and a prolonged recuperation, Robert had arranged for the placement of more than fifteen exchange students from all areas of the world. As well, he and his wife had travelled extensively in South America, often staying with fellow Rotarians he had met through his involvement with student exchange programs. As a result of this contact with South American Rotarians, he had started a small part-time import business that supplies regional retailers with native crafts and artifacts.

"This is more work than working," he remarked, "and I'm a darn sight happier. I've got so many things I want to do that I'm afraid I'll run out of retirement before I run out of things to do! I've just bought a computer but I don't have the time to learn how to use it—yet."

The change that retirement brings is analagous to changes you have already experienced in your life: a career change, a change of spouse, a religious conversion, or dealing with children who grow up and relocate. It is a change that tests your ability to react to new circumstances, to find the silver lining nestled within the cloud of uncertainty.

Retirement will mean one thing for certain. It will mean that some activities you enjoyed and found some meaning in, probably work-related activities, will no longer be available to you. You will be faced with two choices: pining over that loss or seeking out new opportunities to fill the void.

Unfortunately, unless you are already retired, you probably do not have a good perspective on how important your present life circumstances, particularly your employment, are to you. You may not recognize that there will be a void to fill when you retire. You are a victim of the "grass is greener on the other side" syndrome. It is the same illness that afflicts a person anticipating a new job or a new spouse. You are likely to compare the positive aspects of your anticipated retirement to the negative aspects of your current experience. With such a comparsion, your present always comes up second-best.

It is unlikely that your present life circumstances, no matter how unpleasant you judge them to be, provide you with nothing meaningful. It is more likely that they meet *some* inner needs that you have, needs that are important and that will not disappear when you retire. If you want to be happy when you retire, you must seek to understand these needs and to apply this knowledge to your retirement planning.

The basic *You* will not change when you retire. Oh sure, there will be changes, but such changes will come about from how you choose to respond to altered life circumstances, not from any basic change in you. If you are waiting for retirement to make you a better person, be prepared to wait a very long time.

Conventional thinking dominates many of our current ideas about retirement. If you are to believe much of what passes for retirement advice you should get a good financial advisor, pursue southern travel in the winter, engage in "productive" volunteer work during the spring and fall, and maintain your carefully manicured vegetable and flower garden during the summer months—and wait for your Maker in-between!

A problem with such advice, useful as it may be for some people in some sets of circumstances, is that it ignores *you*. It ignores you by pretending to understand what you need in order to be satisfied and then offering a prescription based on that understanding. Another problem with such advice is that it is usually formulated on the basis of some ill-defined concept of what retirement *should* be like—a concept that says, "Your retirement should be like this or that and you should do these things to get there."

For me, *Happily Ever After* is the logical next step after my earlier book, *CareerScan* (Dembner Books, 1985). In *CareerScan*, I rail against current theories of career development that require you to establish long-range life goals and then use logic to plan your life and career based on these goals in a lock-step fashion. It is no more possible or fruitful to establish such a mechanical sequence during your career than it is to follow someone else's advice about how to structure your retirement after your career is over. You will be successful or unsuccessful in your retirement on exactly the same basis as you were successful or unsuccessful in your career—your ability to recognize and respond appropriately to change and opportunity.

Retirement and work are two games with the same set of rules.

Who Should Read This Book?

If you have done any reading in the field of retirement or looked at the library or bookstore shelves for how-to books dealing with retirement planning, you know that there are a great many to choose from. So why read *Happily Ever After*? It is probably poor marketing but let me tell you why not to read this book.

Most self-help books, in the retirement field as in any other, purport to be for everyone—from the indigent grade school dropout to the well-heeled corporate executive. I can make no such claim. *Happily Ever After* is not intended for the individual with little or no work experience, nor is it intended for the individual with extremely limited financial resources for whom day-to-day financial existence will be a sustaining priority. Ideally, the book should be used by those five to ten years from planned retirement, but recent retirees will find much that will apply to their circumstances.

You will find nothing in *Happily Ever After* that will help you plan for your financial future. I have always been better at spending money than saving it and have no secrets that my lawyer would think it safe to share with you about your money.

This book is intended for the reasonably well-educated (formally or self-taught), comfortably affluent, middle-income individual for whom neither lack of money nor severe ill health are prime limiting factors. As my eldest son is quick to remind me, I have spent my career telling yuppies how to get ahead and should now spend my retirement telling aging yuppies how to spend their money. It is hard to get respect from your relatives!

Retirement Planning and You

There are two major components to the psychological side of retirement planning. The first one is akin to the ancient maxim "Know thyself." The second component is related to the first but deals with life's opportunities—how we respond to life's circumstances based on what we know of our needs. These components are important because they occur naturally (I suppose a good psychologist should say unconsciously), whether or not you are aware of them. Successful retirees, and this book is full of their stories, are those who master these components, although many of them have done so "naturally" and are unaware of their own success.

What are *you* like? What demands do you place on the different aspects of your life—work, leisure, family friends—to meet needs that *you* are striving to meet? In the first few chapters of this book I will look at your past as the most reliable way to plan your future. I will focus on helping you to identify the scope of your personal needs, the variety of ways you have met these needs in the past, and the needs that your retirement must meet in order to keep you satisfied.

What opportunities will be available to you when you retire? What is an opportunity, and when is your neighbor's opportunity your pratfall? What problems can you expect in attempting to meet your needs on retirement? In the latter chapters of *Happily Ever After*, I will help you analyze the choices, opportunities, and potential problems that will confront you on retirement. Whether it is moving to sunny Florida or taking on alternative full-time employment, I will look at a method that can help you decide what is right for *you*.

For most people, retirement is something your only go through once, so there is apparently no second chance to do better. But throughout this book I will give you the chance to do just that—albeit second-hand. I will look at profiles of successful retirees to find out what worked and what did not.

Remember that, as in career planning, there are no rules in retirement planning—no "shoulds." There are choices to be made and there are many implications of these choices. What many people find helpful is a method to analyze and expand these choices, to provide a framework that helps them understand the risks and opportunities inherent in any decision. That is the promise of *Happily Ever After*.

Chapter 1

Retirement:
I Love It
—I Hate It

"Take the sum of human achievement in action, in science, in art, in literature—
subtract the work of men above forty, and while we would miss great treasures,
even priceless treasures, we would practically be where we are today. . . . The
effective moving, vitalizing of the world is done between the ages of twenty-five
and forty."

—William Osler, *The Fixed Period*

When I showed an early draft of *Happily Ever After* to a friend, a
writer and media go-between for a large government agency, she
winced—quite noticeably I thought—at the notion of retiring.
Marge is bright, articulate, well educated, and well paid—and still
she finds the thought of what she calls "imminent uselessness"
frightening. "Sure," she chided me, "it's okay for you," and then
added only half in jest, "You've never worked. Why would *you*
worry about retiring?"

Hoping that I could recover my manuscript before she took
complete leave of her faculties, I did my best to feign surprise at the
transparent honesty of her observation. "Not work???" I repeated,
my voice trailing upwards in my best indignant style.

Ignoring my righteous indignation, Marge stumbled on, "You
know what I mean—never really worked *for* anyone. If you've
never worked for anyone, how could you possibly retire from
working for anyone?"

Hoping my university employers were not recording this conversation, I thought it best to let her continue this line of thought
through to its ultimate illogical conclusion, not that I had much
choice in the matter anyway.

"Retirement is when you are finished working for someone. It's when you reach the end of the road and they pension you off," Marge repeated with not a little uncertainty. "You've always worked for yourself, or at least you always acted like you worked for yourself, so it's no big deal for you."

It was the "acted like" part that really got me, so, settling myself in for one of her "tell it like it really is" lectures on life, I begged her to continue.

"I have this theory that the closer your real life is to your retirement, the easier it will be to retire," she said, looking as confused as I was beginning to feel. "I mean, if I was a housewife and had stayed home for the past thirty years, it would be nothing to retire. It's almost like I would have already been retired so I wouldn't know the difference."

Using my best psychologist nonjudgmental paraphrasing techniques, I allowed as to how, if you did not *feel* there were any differences, there probably were not any differences. She took this to be agreement and carried on.

"It's the thought of everything going at once that really gets me— it just seems so uncertain," she added. "I've always wanted to be free of the nine-to-five regimen of work, but what's really going to happen? How am I going to handle it—not working, free time, husband hanging around all the time, getting old? Besides that, this place is easy. I *know* what to do, even when I don't want to do it. There's a strange kind of security in that."

"There's a Strange Kind of Security in That"

Like Marge, there are two components to the thinking of many of us who approach retirement—begrudging appreciation of our present life circumstances and uncertainty of our postretirement expectations. Your present life circumstances may be unfulfilling but they are predictable—at least more predictable than the future. You may be unhappy—but at least you know how unhappy you are. It is this *knowledge* of your present state of affairs, and the *lack of knowledge* about the future, that pulls you in one direction while it pushes you in another.

Patrick, fifty-eight, a well-to-do owner of a three-office commercial real estate operation wanted to retire—at least he was making all the right noises about retirement. He had been in the business since he was twenty, working with his uncle for the first ten years before a family squabble forced him to start his own, very successful operation.

Patrick had very nearly retired on a buy-out basis the year earlier but had backed out at the last minute with imagined concerns about the security of the financial package. The owner-to-be had then purchased one of Patrick's competitors and had done very well in the local market—mainly at Patrick's expense.

Now, Patrick had another offer in hand, one that by his own admission seemed to be based on the strength of his company a year earlier rather than the current weakened position. And still he hesitated. "I know it seems good, probably too good, but I still don't know if I should take it," he commented in an interview. "Maybe a person like me shouldn't retire. All I really know is real estate."

By external standards, Patrick had all the attributes for a successful retirement—money, good health, stable family—and still he hesitated. Why?

Like Marge and Patrick, you may find that you have very mixed feelings about retirement. On the one hand, you are able to analyze the future, calculate probabilities, and tell yourself that everything *should* be fine. On a more emotional level, the butterflies in your stomach are yelling, "Don't believe it. Something will screw up!" It is difficult to get the butterflies to speak a language your head understands—or vice versa.

You probably have only limited choices about whether or not you will retire. You may have some limited decision-making ability as to *when* you will retire and the form such retirement will take, but you will probably retire from your conventional full-time job within a very limited age-time band, like it or not.

In addition to "normal" retirements at, say, age sixty or sixty-five, early retirements and, more commonly, "voluntary" forced retirements are on the increase. Such early retirements are necessitated by a rapidly changing work environment, reduction in the required labor force, and the desire to replace older, more expensive workers with less expensive younger and/or part-time labor. In many situations, retirement is not an option—it is a necessity.

Increasingly, over the past ten years, some individuals have rebelled against the notion of forced retirement and have sought solace in the law. Feeling that their human or civil rights were violated by notions of forced retirement, such individuals have argued that mandatory retirement should be an issue of competence rather than age. However, even recent changes in the law are projected to have only a minimal effect on the average age of retirement. There is little evidence that employers—to some extent with the tacit support of organized labor—will not find alternative means to effect retirement, although under a different label or by different means.

In all retirement situations, whether voluntary or forced, there are many personal decisions to be made. What will you do? Where will you live? How will you replace the part that work has assumed in your life? How can you keep from being bored silly?

The personal decisions surrounding retirement are no different from the personal decisions that have characterized your life thus far. The common thread that binds such decisions is *compromise*. It is the compromise based on the truism that there is no perfect decision waiting "out there" for you to find, that every decision, no matter how well considered, has risks. It is the courage to act *in spite of this uncertainty* that characterizes those who are successful—in retirement as in most other aspects of life.

If you have been happy or satisfied in our life before retirement, you have all of the ammunition you need to ensure a successful and a meaningful retirement. Luckily, even if you have not had a particularly happy or satisfied life before retirement, you can *still* have a satisfying retirement. In either case, you will not *necessarily* have the same kind of retirement as the life that preceded retirement. Success in retirement is not a matter of duplicating the past, nor is it a matter of luck—it is a matter of *choice*.

Retirement is a fresh start—yours!

In many ways, the transition from paid work to retirement parallels other transitions that you have made in your life—the transition from grade school to high school, from high school to college, from single to married, from childless to parent, from parent to grandparent. You can probably think of some people who did very well at one stage but failed miserably at the next—the high school scholar and socialite who bombed out of college academically and personally. At the same time you can probably recall others who were miserable failures at one stage but who excelled at the next—the shy adolescent who blossomed into a successful bank executive or the day-dreaming student who went on to build a successful small business. Retirement is a lot like that. It is difficult to tell who will be a winner or a loser until it is over!

If you are to retire, by your own decision or as a result of a decision taken by others, there is one overwhelmingly important rule to keep in mind. For retirement to be a satisfying time of life, it must result in you going *to* something. It cannot simply be retirement *from* paid work. No matter how unimportant you judge your present work life to be, it does provide you with something. If you simply remove that something, without replacing it with something else, hopefully a better something else, you will be a net loser.

Retirement happiness = (Impact of new experiences) − (Impact of what you leave behind)

The skills and personal characteristics you have acquired thus far in your life will only be useful if you recognize their worth in the new situations you will face. This recognition means coming to grips with you—recognizing what you are as well as what you are not—and using this knowledge as a guide in decisions you will be required to make. It is not that these new decisions will be any more difficult that ones you have already encountered. But they will be *different* and that is the crux of the retirement problem.

It is this *difference* that throws many people off the track to a meaningful retirement. They reason that what worked before will work again and spend a good deal of fruitless thrashing about in seeking to re-live something that is over, to *mimic* the past rather than using that past as a springboard to a better future. Put simply, what you have done in the past is of little consequence—*why you have done it* is paramount. It is the understanding of this "why" that is the essence of this first section of *Happily Ever After*.

Chapter 2

Needs or "Why You Done It"

"Things are seldom what they seem."
—W. S. Gilbert, *H.M.S. Pinafore*

"Today is the first day of the rest of your life!" How often have you heard this glib assertion, whether in a corporate or religious pep talk, motivational speech, or inspired conversation with a friend? It has a seducing ring, doesn't it, one that practically begs agreement? There is something compelling in thinking that it is possible to make a truly fresh start, to forget the past with its mistakes and inadequacies, to forge ahead with a clean slate. The unfortunate thing is though it may be compelling, it is also dead wrong.

It was George Santayana who once said that those who are ignorant of the past were doomed to repeat it. I am certain that Santayana meant the heroic past—wars or pestilences of one kind of another—when he coined his oft-quoted maxim. But it is a maxim that is particularly appropriate for individual history. In planning any aspect of your future life, you forget your past at your peril.

To replace one maxim with another, today is not the first day of the rest of your life—it is the last day of the life you have had so far! The last day of your past successes and failures, high points and depressions. If you do not want to repeat your past (and if you are contemplating retirement you hardly have time for that), you must turn your past to profit. You must *use* your past to give you a head start in planning for your future. You must seek to understand what your past tells about *you*. Then and only then will you be in the position to capitalize on—not ignore—what has gone before.

Even when the past has not been wholly forgotten, there is a tendency on the part of some people to shun it as a reminder of bygone inadequacies. After all, they reason, if the past has not been happy, of what use can it be in planning for a happier future? What can you learn about fishing from a snarled casting reel?

Your past has one saving grace—it is over. You do not have to guess about whether or not you *would* enjoy it, *might* find it meaningful, or *could* profit from it. It is all there, like it or not, behind you. In fact, using your past is like betting on last week's horse-race results—unexciting but accurate. And, like that horse race, although you can never run last week's race over again, there is a great deal to learn about the horse from looking at old race results. Horses may never run the same as they did before but they never run totally differently either!

Many people ignore the past, not out of a conscious well-measured decision, but rather because of the apparent hopelessness in analyzing a confused jumble of seemingly unrelated events, separated by many years, in a manner that leads anywhere. The past is so b-i-g that its very size becomes more of a problem than the anticipated benefit of using it for future planning. How do you combine or summarize something that big? How do you calculate an "average" for your life?

Undoubtedly, your past combines many things, many events that are thrown together like a pre-payday soup. There are things that are important to you, others that are trivial or banal. The difficulty is not one of remembering the scattered things you have done through the course of your life. It is in finding the meaning that is scattered across many events occuring over an extended time. The difficulty is in finding the meat in the soup!

In planning your retirement, you must capitalize on your past if you are to maximize your future.

Needs and You

It is one thing to assert the importance of using your past to help you plan for your future—your retirement—but it is quite another thing to actually do it. To make it easier you will have to look at some basic principles that have to do with human motivation, with needs and needs satisfaction. But first things first. What are *needs*?

Needs range from the basic physical human requirements that we all share to more sophisticated or "psychological" preferences. Needs are inner forces that drive us to action in order to be satisfied. On a physiological level the need for food drives you to your lunch bucket or a restaurant. On a psychological level, the need for companionship may drive you into intense personal relationships, service clubs, or volunteer work. In each case, the goal is *satisfaction* or reduction in the driving force of the need.

We all have much the same physiological needs; food, shelter, safety, and the like. In fact, until these physiological needs have been met to a sufficient degree, the more psychological needs do not attain prominence. On a relative basis, it is difficult to be overly concerned about not having a sufficient degree of meaningful contact with others when you must be concerned with dodging bullets or finding a dry place to sleep at night.

Once you get beyond these basic physical needs, there is a whole range of needs that is different for each one of us, different not so much in kind as in degree. One person may "need" more physical activity, another more companionship with others, or another more artistic expression. Although it is probably safe to say that all people demonstrate all possible needs to *some* degree, the differences in degree of need between individuals are far more important than this basic theoretical similarity. It is this difference that contributes to making you uniquely you.

Once you have reached adulthood, your needs are pretty well established. Without going into the unresolved debates about heredity versus environment in the development of human needs—debates that have plagued psychology since its origins—suffice it to say that, however your needs developed, they are quite stable by middle adulthood at the latest. What changes through adulthood are the *opportunities* that are available to meet your various needs and the *relative apparent strengths* of various needs dependent on how each one is being satisfied at any given moment in time. Let us look at these two factors in turn.

In terms of the opportunities available to meet your needs, there is a strange quirk of being human in that needs that are largely satisfied do not feel like needs at all. This is true even for those needs that, if they were not being met, would be extremely compelling in their "push to action," what psychologists call motivation. It is only when the circumstances that allow for the satisfaction of such a need change dramatically that awareness of the need becomes obvious. In such circumstances, the individual so affected thrashes about, often in real desperation, seeking something that will reduce the driving power of the need that is no longer being met.

Needs are important because the satisfaction of your needs on an ongoing basis is crucial to your ongoing happiness.

Jeff, fifty-five, a plant biotechnology expert at a mid-sized western university, had just been forced into early retirement as a result of budget cutbacks by his employer. Jeff had been economically self-sufficient since he was forty, the result of shrewd real estate and stocks acquisitions made since he had graduated from college. In some ways, he looked forward to retirement since work was very demanding of his time, and he had considered quitting more than once because he "didn't need the money."

Four months after leaving his job, Jeff found himself very much "at loose ends." He had managed his personal holdings about as much as they could stand and sometimes found himself hoping that things would go wrong so that he could get involved in fixing them up.

"I think I miss setting up a whole program, getting involved in all the various steps, and then seeing the whole thing come out," he said in one of our infrequent consultations. "Everything I do now can run just fine without me. I can't just collect rent and clip investment coupons for the rest of my life."

The *relative apparent strengths* of your needs is a phenomenon closely related to the opportunities available to meet your needs. Very often you are driven to action by needs that, on an absolute basis, are secondary. However, these secondary needs seem stronger than more primary needs you have because you are doing very little to satisfy them. For example, you may know individuals who are driven by the desire for money or other economic assets. But you know too that these same individuals often sing a different tune when their health, or that of a loved one, is threatened. Money, or the driving power of amassing wealth, takes a back seat to a stronger need (security or health) when the satisfaction of that stronger need is threatened.

The relative apparent strengths of your needs are very important to the decision-making process you undertake in evaluating needs satisfaction *opportunities* that are available to you on a day-to-day basis. A common foible of human decision-making in evaluating opportunities is to place undue weight on secondary needs that are not being met at the current time to the detriment of stronger needs that are being met (and thus may not feel like needs!).

Often, the result of such lop-sided decision-making is choosing a course of action that helps to satisfy the secondary need while at the same time neglecting the primary need that was previously being satisfied. In such circumstances, the decision-maker often ends up unhappier than before the decision-making started—albeit for different reasons! As we will see later, it need not end up this way.

During his last three years of employment, Jacques had looked forward to his retirement. The popular regional director of an international union, he was constantly in the limelight, traveled a good deal, and had a very active business-social life.

"When I retire, I'm going to buy a little farm, settle down, and just do nothin' for the first five years, and then I'm going to get real lazy," Jacques used to say jokingly when asked about his retirement. When he retired, he did just that.

For the first six months Jacques could not have been more happy with his retirement—or so it seemed. He puttered around the farm, planted a small vegetable garden, seldom went anywhere or did anything. The few friends who did see him in his self-imposed isolation often remarked that he did not seem like the same person.

Gradually, after the novelty of the first six months had worn off, Jacques seemed increasingly uneasy with his retirement decision. He frequently drove to the city, often with nothing to do once he got there and began to "drop in" to his old office at coffee times or just before lunch. To his wife's surprise, he had broached the idea of relocating in the city and securing part-time consulting work.

The grass is always greener on the other side—from either side of the fence!

When you are considering your needs, it is important to remember that they are *neither good nor bad* although there are undoubtedly good and bad behaviors done in the name of every need. Needs simply *are*, and as adults, we seem to have very little influence on the nature or strength of our needs. Rather, our influence or control is limited to choosing how we will seek to meet our needs—and that is a big enough job on its own!

A Compendium of Needs

Psychologists have tried for many years to identify all of the human needs that exert driving forces on human behavior. If one were to be uncharitable, it could be said that this labeling has done little other than to increase the weight of most dictionaries or psychology textbooks. As will become clearer in the next chapter, some form of categorization is useful, particularly if you do not become overly concerned about the exclusivity of each category or think that you have labeled all possible needs.

The critical thing about the relationship between needs and behavior is that everything is very idiosyncratic. Different individuals can do the same thing for widely different reasons. As well, there is often more than one need satisfied by a particular behavior. That is what makes the process of needs identification so difficult—and so interesting. But, I am getting ahead of myself. Let us look at your needs before we look at your behavior.

Below is a list many people have found useful in terms of their career and retirement planning. This list of human needs includes most of the important driving forces that typify adults' work and nonwork behavior. I will describe these needs in this chapter and explain their use in the retirement planning process in later chapters.

In looking at these definitions of different needs remember that the important thing is *not* simply whether or not you have done activities such as the examples provided but whether or not such activities were meaningful to you—whether or not you found such activity *personally meaningful* at the time or in hindsight.

At this point, do not confuse yourself by thinking "I would have enjoyed it *if* I had done it." While that *might* be true, right now we are only focusing on your needs as exemplified by your *actual past behavior that you have found personally meaningful.*

1. INFLUENCE

You like to be in a position to change the attitudes or alter the opinions of others.

This is often a difficult need to assess because, as a society, we often denigrate those who are open about their need for influence. This usually means that individuals still pursue activities that will satisfy their Influence needs but they often do so under the guise of other, more socially acceptable needs, such as Altruism.

Personal Preferences to Look For:

(a) You enjoy being asked for advice by others and find pleasure in providing such information.
(b) When policy is being planned for a group, you prefer to take an active part in developing it.
(c) You enjoy participating in discussions with others where you are able to put forward your beliefs and opinions.
(d) In a situation where a group of people has to do something, you enjoy the role of leader more than follower.
(e) You enjoy public speaking, corporate or family management, or volunteer work in which you guide others.
(f) It is important to you that you are able to convince others of beliefs or values you hold to be important.

2. ALTRUISM

It is important for you to help other people by your actions, either alone or in groups.

This is also a difficult need to identify because frequently a helping act is not done exclusively for helping reasons but for other reasons such as Influence or Competition. Often it is a revelation to individuals to discover that actions they have undertaken, often very positive and helping actions, were *not* done exclusively out of a sense of altruism. This in no way discounts the importance or meaningfulness of their actions but does give a different perspective to the motivation that drove them to undertake the act. It is sometimes hard to keep in mind that needs are amoral—no need is inherently better than another.

Personal Preferences to Look For:

(a) You enjoy being part of "worthy causes," of attempting to help others by your actions.
(b) You feel that it is important to contribute part of your earnings to charities in order to help others.
(c) You get upset with people who always seem to "look out for Number One."
(d) You worry about the underdog and would like to do what you can to help.
(e) You volunteer on occasion to help other people without thought of personal gain.
(f) You feel good about contributing your efforts or resources to assist others in some way.

3. AFFILIATION

You desire feelings of closeness and similarity with a group of people or an organization. The need for Affiliation is concerned with the camaraderie experienced by working with others or being in close association with others in a nonwork situation.

Affiliation is a need that we sometimes take for granted because it is often satisfied by our day-to-day life. Sometimes it is only possible to get a clear idea of its importance when we are placed in a situation where meeting the need is impossible. Situations such as working exclusively at home or in the electronic office both have a common thread—minimal opportunity to meet an Affiliation need.

Personal Preferences to Look For:

(a) You feel more comfortable working on a task as part of a group rather than individually.
(b) You have developed strong ties or feelings of loyalty for organizations you were part of.
(c) In nonwork endeavors as well as work, you enjoy group activities rather than wholly individual pursuits.

(d) You enjoy being around others, the feeling you are part of a group.

(e) You enjoy pursuing activities not so much because of what you are doing, but because these activities are done with others.

(f) You experience "cabin fever" when you must work or play on your own for extended periods.

4. COMPETITION

You find it pleasurable to engage in activities where you are trying to outperform others. This would also include behavior where you are trying to reach or better some internal benchmark or standard that you have established which may not involve direct face-to-face competition with others. Competition is a need that, although most people have it to a higher degree than they are willing to admit, is often not talked about in polite company.

Personal Preferences to Look For:

(a) You enjoy participating in competitive events such as sports, games, contests, etc.

(b) You have difficulty accepting losing in events that have a win-lose dimension.

(c) You perform best in situations where you can gauge your progress against that of others even if there is no "head to head" race involved.

(d) You like to be judged by results rather than by what you do to achieve those results.

(e) You find yourself setting standards against which you judge your own performance.

5. INTELLECT

You achieve feelings of satisfaction by thinking through problems or developing courses of action. This need might be met, not by actually doing the task, but by planning and organizing the doing of the task. Very often, the Intellect need is met in doing a new activity for the first time rather than repetitively. In contrast to the many needs that are met by repeated actions, this need presents a special challenge. Once an activity is learned or a solution is outlined, repeating the event again and again no longer meets the need and a new task must be found.

Personal Preferences to Look For:

(a) You enjoy solving problems, particularly difficult ones that you have not dealt with before.
(b) You are more likely to enjoy planning how you would do something than going through the steps of doing it.
(c) You get few feelings of accomplishment from doing routine things where you already know how to do them.
(d) You enjoy working at new activities and may become bored quickly.
(e) Difficult problems challenge you and provide real enjoyment in their solution.

6. AESTHETICS

Appreciation of things of beauty is meaningful for you. Aesthetic needs could be met by everything from ditch digging to mathematics and is related to the feeling of peace or internal orderliness derived from interacting with a thing of beauty. This is a need that is often confused with artistic ability—it is not that. In fact, practicing artists would not necessarily manifest this need any more than anyone else and could be motivated by far more pragmatic concerns.

Personal Preferences to Look For:

(a) You got pleasure from viewing works of art or literature.
(b) You are able to express yourself by making things that may have little utilitarian value.
(c) You actively seek out artistic or literary encounters such as exhibitions, theater, nature, etc.
(d) You are most satisfied when you work or play in an aesthetically pleasing environment.
(e) You get satisfaction from painting, sculpture, music, cooking, writing, or other similar activities.

7. SECURITY

It is important for your happiness that you are certain as to how things are going and your place in them. It is easy to feel like your need for Security is in conflict with other needs that you have and it is easy to mistakenly assume that you must choose security *or* insecurity. Like many other needs, Security is easier to identify in its absence than its presence.

Personal Preferences to Look For:

(a) You are most comfortable when you have established a routine.
(b) Even if things are going somewhat badly, you find it difficult to try something new and untried.
(c) You prefer moderate guaranteed long-term rewards to greater but riskier short-term rewards.
(d) You are most productive when you feel safe and secure.
(e) You feel most comfortable when you are in total control of events around you.
(f) You are more likely to make an error of omission rather than one of commission in your personal life.

8. RECOGNITION

Doing things viewed as important by others is important for you. Once again, Recognition is a need that we usually do not talk openly about even though our need for it is evident to those around us.

Personal Preferences to Look For:

(a) You enjoy "putting on a show" for others or demonstrating that you can do something that might surprise others.
(b) You enjoy success most when others see your accomplishments.
(c) You prefer it when people with whom you are associated notice how well you do things.
(d) You might find yourself doing something you do not particularly enjoy so that others will comment favorably.
(e) You feel happiest when you are in the "limelight."
(f) You willingly participate in activities such as service clubs, church leadership, or political activity.

9. ADVENTURE

You desire change, a fast pace, and excitement in things you do. Although this is perhaps a more socially acceptable need (certainly on the cocktail party circuit it is), and on an absolute basis it may be quite modest in strength, it is one need we frequently overestimate. The Adventure need often feels stronger on a relative basis because there is so little opportunity for most of us to satisfy it in our everyday lives. It can be a powerful motivator—but, unchecked, a dangerous one.

Personal Preferences to Look For:

(a) You tire of routine things rather quickly.
(b) You enjoy doing things that are risky just for the joy of doing them.

(c) You find that you must keep yourself "revved up" in order to be productive.

(d) The less things are the same day-after-day, the more you enjoy it.

(e) You seek risk in your hobbies or are most comfortable in high-risk employment.

(f) You begin to feel uneasy once you have everything in your life working smoothly.

10. FREEDOM

It is important for you to be free from constraints imposed by others. Freedom needs are satisfied through a state of mind in that the important thing is that you feel you are free. This might be accomplished in situations where others would feel confined.

Personal Preferences to Look For:

(a) It is important that you set your own rules.

(b) You find it hard to be productive when somebody else tells you what to do, even if it is the same thing you would have done yourself.

(c) You are happiest when others make no demands on you.

(d) You find yourself wanting to "throw everything in" and start over, even when you are successful.

11. MATERIALISM

You enjoy amassing money or other assets. You gain pleasure from using or reflecting upon what you have accumulated. Although the Materialism need is related to other needs such as Recognition and Influence, it is important enough to be considered on its own. Often, what seems like a need for Materialism is not that. Rather, it reflects a need for Security, or Influence, or Freedom. It is possible to satisfy these needs without Materialism or vice versa, and it is quite important to distinguish the need for Materialism from these other needs in undertaking your own needs analysis.

Personal Preferences to Look For:

(a) You work mainly to obtain economic benefits.
(b) Success is gauged in terms of the "bottom line" as far as you are concerned.
(c) You enjoy making money, even when you do not need it for any particular purpose.
(d) It would be hard for you to be "poor but happy."
(e) You enjoy having things, even though you cannot identify an immediate use for them.

12. RELIGION

It is important for you to adhere to a set of religious or moral principles. It is not necessary that this need be met through interaction with an organized religion. Rather, satisfaction is related to motivation by a "higher power" or set of moral principles.

Personal Preferences to Look For:

(a) You find great meaning in the spiritual side of life.
(b) It is important to you that you actually practice your religion on a day-by-day basis.
(c) You find comfort in being able to relate your activities to a higher dimension.
(d) Religion is the one part of your life that keeps you going.

When you read through this list of needs you will probably find yourself thinking that you have all of them—and you are right! To some extent, all of us have all needs. Where we differ is in the *relative intensity* of the various needs and the manner we have chosen to act out these needs in our everyday lives. In looking through the list above do not just ask yourself whether or not you have each need. Ask yourself *how often*, in relative terms, you have found yourself doing things that are indicative of each need.

Although you can probably think of a great number of other more specific needs than the twelve listed, they could probably be included under one or another of these general categories. The need for social contact, for example, could be categorized under Affiliation or Altruism.

Although in defining needs I treat them as separate and distinct from one another, that is seldom the case in real life. It is the rule, not the exception, for one behavior or thing that you do to be indicative of more than one need. For example, you might enjoy being appointed to the executive position of your service or social association because it satisfies a need for Altruism, Influence, Competition, and Affiliation. Or, it might satisfy your need for Freedom in allowing you to be more free from the constraints of your family.

In determining your needs, "why" you did something is as important as "what you did."

It is not possible to identify your needs from any single life experience no matter how important that experience might be. To provide such guidance you need to focus on the bigger picture; you need to calculate that elusive "average" for your life by focusing on a number of meaningful life events together with understanding the reasons such events were important for you. In this way, you will be using your past to understand your present and improve your future.

It is difficult to identify your needs from a set of definitions, difficult because you find yourself wanting to have certain needs based on the definitions. At this point, do not worry about whether or not you have each of the needs cited, or the strength of each need. I will look at a reliable way to do just that in later chapters. At this point, be satisfied in making certain that you understand what is meant by the various needs.

Your needs are a vital link to planning your retirement. They are vital because you will not be happy or satisfied in your retirement unless you can orchestrate a retirement that allows you to meet your needs. You do this by planning a retirement around activities that are designed to do just that. But, first things first. What are your needs and how can you be certain that you have identified them accurately?

Chapter 3

Using Your Past
to Improve
Your Future

"Life can only be understood backwards;
but it must be lived forwards."
—Søren Kierkegaard, *Life*

The best way to assess your needs is to use a method that helps you to interpret information from your past in such a way as to identify the needs you will seek to meet in the future. The method that I will outline uses *behaviors* or *actions* that you have exhibited in the past to help you to identify your needs or "motivators for action." Using this method will help you to discover for yourself the hidden meaning of your important past experiences or *meaningful life events* and provide you with the information you will need to plan a meaningful retirement.

Understanding your past is the best way to improve your future.

The way to use your previous life events to ascertain your needs is to start with a number of examples of things you have done throughout the course of your life that you found to be important or meaningful to you. Such events are *not necessarily accomplishments* in that they may not reflect extraordinary talent, effort, or initiative. They need not have been difficult or out of the ordinary in any way. As well, your examples can be from any area of your life, work or nonwork, paid or unpaid. In fact, it is a good idea to identify examples from all aspects of your life since your work alone probably has not given you sufficient opportunity to meet all of your needs.

Examples of meaningful life events might be winning an oratorical contest in grade six, establishing a sexual relationship with someone you found highly desirable, earning a promotion, enjoying a particular holiday with the family, solving difficult crossword puzzles, planning a new business venture, or the like. The only critical thing in any example you choose is that the event be *meaningful* to you.

In using your past actions to identify your needs you should purposely ignore your abilities. While it might be important, for other reasons, for purposes of identifying your needs, it is not important how well you did something. It is solely important how *meaningful* or *important* that activity was to you. For example, you may have done extraordinarily well in college, achieving grades that were the envy of your peers. At the same time, you might judge this to be unimportant, something you did because you had to do it or because it was required to obtain a license to practice your profession. Conversely, you might have done rather poorly at college but enjoyed the process immensely because of the social aspects or joy of learning new material. The first instance speaks clearly to your skills—you can do well even when you are not particularly interested in something. The second instance, because it deals with an experience that is *meaningful* to you, would be indicative of the kind of experience that can help you to identify your needs. It is your needs that are important to your retirement planning.

For purposes of illustration, let us look at the examples provided by George, a participant in a retirement planning seminar I conducted several years ago.

George was a fifty-five-year-old English teacher who was considering retirement on a "thirty years and out" plan recently agreed to by his employer. His partial list of personally important life events included:

1. Ten years ago, as senior committee member, George designed a revised grade ten English curriculum. He then taught several workshops on a regional basis outlining the new program to his fellow teachers. The feedback he had received from this experience was very positive and had earned him some measure of a regional reputation in his field.
2. An avid recreational sailor, George had won the local sailing competition for more years than he could remember. He was especially proud that he had coached his eldest son to win the event three years ago, beating George in the final eliminations.
3. In his final year of high school he was chosen by his fellow students to be class spokesperson during a dispute with a difficult teacher. He enjoyed doing it even though he felt it had resulted in his losing the school English scholarship later that year.
4. George had successfully completed a self-study course in home winemaking and had his first batch ready for tasting at Christmas during a large family reunion.
5. George had been asked to apply for administrative positions with his school jurisdiction on several occasions although he had declined each time.
6. Although he maintained that he was sorry, George remembered (with a gleam in his eye) that he had pilfered hubcaps as a teenager and was never caught.
7. He had stayed "successfully married" to the same woman for twenty-eight years even though many of his friends were on their second or third go-round.
8. During college, he had toured Europe with a friend on a very sparse budget. He particularly liked seeing how far he could go with very little money and meeting new people.
9. George had been selected "Teacher of the Year" on three occasions during his career.
10. He had saved very scrupulously during his first fifteen years

of employment and was able to completely pay for his house in record time.

11. During college, George had tutored a deaf student in reading skills. That student had subsequently graduated from a first-class technical institute and done very well. Twenty years later he still corresponded with George on an irregular basis.

12. Never a great team player, George had "forced" himself to join an "old timer" basketball league comprised of teachers and their friends. To his own surprise, he had thoroughly enjoyed himself.

13. While in his forties, George had maintained a secretive three-year affair with a much younger woman. Although he claimed to feel guilty about the relationship he did rate it as one of the more important events of his life.

14. George's daughter had just given birth to his first grandchild and he found that he enjoyed this new experience a great deal.

15. George had done very well financially during his career, orchestrating a modest income into a substantial holding compared to that of other teachers.

In identifying your own examples, err on the side of being too specific rather than too general. It is too general to say "raising my family" and is better if you can think of one or several unique instances of raising your family that were especially meaningful to you. A good rule of thumb is that you should be able to close your eyes and picture yourself doing the event or that others should be able to do so if you describe the event to them. It is difficult to picture "raising a family" in the general sense although it is possible to picture a variety of specific events associated with doing so.

It is impossible to be too specific in specifying your important life experiences.

RETIREMENT EXERCISE 1

Take a plain sheet of paper and write down *two* things you have done in your life thus far that are important to you.

Before you go on to identify other things you have done or experienced in your life, look carefully at your first two examples. It is usual to be somewhat hesitant in identifying your experiences. You may feel comfortable to identify only those things that are very socially acceptable or accomplishments that are not personally meaningful. Either of these errors results in getting a "doctored" picture of yourself, a little like using an airbrush to patch up the family portrait. Since it is only you that will see this information there is no reason to be selective in identifying your examples.

It is most useful in the needs identification process if you can identify a good number of examples—fifteen to twenty examples should be your minimum goal. As you will see later, it is only by *averaging across examples* that you are really able to get a reliable measure of your needs. Experience indicates that with any less than fifteen to twenty examples you are in danger of putting too much emphasis on any one example.

In searching for happiness in your future life, look first to the meaning of your past life.

Before you go on to identify other important life experiences you have had, read through the example below.

Marcia was a sixty-year-old accountant for a multinational oil company. She had been employed full time for the past twenty-three years (since her children had reached school age) and on a part-time basis previously. Her list of important life events included:

1. Although she had worked full time for only three years before quitting to have children, Marcia was especially proud that her firm had thought enough of her performance to offer her another full-time position nine years later, when her children had reached school age.

2. Marcia was an accomplished musician and had played the bassoon with her local symphony for many years. She enjoyed the challenge of playing with younger people, some of whom were professional musicians, and she remembered with pride the twenty-five-year service plaque that had been presented to her at the conclusion of the previous year's season.

3. During her "dating years," Marcia had been very popular as well as strikingly beautiful. She indicated that this had been very important for her at the time and she remembered this with much fondness many years later.

4. Marcia had been very active with a local voluntary organization that dealt with girls without mothers. She particularly enjoyed her work extending over a seven-year term with a troubled adolescent who had progressed to a much less troubled young woman.

5. For a period of five years, Marcia had taught an evening accounting class for her local community college and had enjoyed it very much.

6. Marcia was the financial manager for the investments of her husband and herself. Although a very conservative individual, she was very consistent and enduring, building a sizeable "nest egg" over a thirty-year period. She looked on this with a good deal of pride.

7. Marcia had enjoyed her children very much. She especially remembered two events: the marriage of her eldest daughter and the graduation from high school of her son, who was not a good student.

8. Marcia's husband was an avid fisherman and she accom-

panied him on many of his weekend and holiday trips. Although she was only modestly interested in fishing at the beginning, this interest had grown over the years. As well, she noted that "it's hard to avoid talking to each other when you're sitting together in the middle of a lake."

9. Marcia had been active in politics at the local level. She particularly enjoyed her involvement as the treasurer and executive member of the campaign committee for a successful mayoralty candidate in her home town.

10. Marcia had gone through some "emotional problems" when she was in her early fifties and reported that her involvement with her church and a self-help group associated with her church was instrumental in her improvement.

11. Marcia had been present at the deaths of both her father and mother, and although it had been upsetting, she regarded these as very important points in her life.

12. During high school, Marcia had been very active (and effective) at public speaking, an area she regretted not being more involved in during her later life.

13. Over the course of her long career with the oil company, Marcia had been involved in several large-scale system changes, including two different computerizations. She had enjoyed these substantial disruptions although they were very demanding when they occurred.

14. While in their late forties, Marcia and her husband had designed and built their own home. Although, at the time, the project had nearly driven them both crazy, Marcia was proud of what they had done together—and with the result.

15. Marcia was one of the first women employed by her oil-company employer to be promoted to a middle management position. She was very proud of this.

RETIREMENT EXERCISE 1—*continued*

It is time to put pencil to paper again and identify more examples. Remember, they do not have to be earth shattering in significance. They must only be important to you. Do not worry that your examples do not come easily or in great abundance. It is very typical to think of one or two examples and then experience a "dry spell" before thinking of others. It is not unusual to average thirty minutes per example. Aim for fifteen or more examples.

Putting Your Life Examples to Work

If you have been diligent in reporting your fifteen or twenty life examples, you should breathe a deep sigh of relief. In my experience, most people report that the remembering and recording process you have just completed is the single most difficult part of their needs identification process. In fact, if you have come through this process in less than three to five hours, you are exceptional!

It is one thing to identify the things in your past life that have been important. It is quite another to find the meaning hidden in these important life events. To discover this meaning, you must move from remembering *what* you did through to identifying *why* you did what you did, and you must end up using this information to help you identify or label your needs. Your life events are not so very important in and of themselves. They are important only because of what these experiences tell you about yourself by virtue of your having enjoyed doing them.

Remember that having enjoyed something is proof positive that whatever you did was meeting your needs. When you identify why your memorable life experiences were meaningful you will have the necessary data to compose a true picture of yourself—a picture that will enable you to infer your long-term life needs. To plan your retirement future, *you need this picture.*

The importance of your past actions is in the validity they lend to your planning for the future.

I will demonstrate this process with the example of George, our soon-to-be-retired teacher, introduced earlier in this chapter.

When George looked over his list of important life events he was surprised at the consistencies as well as the apparent conflicts in reasons he identified as to why these events were important to him. Perhaps more importantly, he found the consistency of the "Needs Met" by his important life events a real eye-opener.

Events/Past Actions	Significance	Needs Met
1. Ten years ago, as senior committee member, George designed a revised grade ten English curriculum. He then taught several workshops on a regional basis outlining the new program to his fellow teachers. The feedback he had received from this experience was very positive and had earned him some measure of a regional reputation in his field.	"I didn't particularly enjoy working with the planning committee in charge of the curriculum design but I did enjoy completing the parts of the revision I was solely responsible for. It was difficult but perhaps more enjoyable because of this difficulty. . . . I especially enjoyed leading the workshops for the other teachers because it gave me the chance to 'perform.' Maybe I'm just a frustrated actor," he remarked.	Influence Intellect Recognition

Events/Past Actions	Significance	Needs Met
2. An avid recreational sailor, George had won the local sailing competition for more years than he could remember. But, he was especially proud that he had coached his eldest son to win the event three years ago, beating George in the final eliminations.	"Sailing," said George, "is one of the few things I do where you know immediately when you've made a mistake. Besides, it makes me feel good to let the 'white pants and blazer set' know that somebody else can sail better than they can."	Competition Influence Recognition Affiliation
3. In his final year of high school he was chosen by his fellow students to be class spokesperson during a dispute with a difficult teacher. He enjoyed doing it even though he felt it had resulted in his losing the school English scholarship later that year.	Although a good student, George was a shy boy during high school and he was surprised to be asked to talk to the teacher. "I didn't think I could do it but I was too proud to tell them that so I just went ahead and talked to her," he said. "The teacher seemed surprised that I could be that tenacious."	Recognition Affiliation Adventure
4. George had successfully completed a self-study course in home winemaking and had his first batch ready for tasting at Christmas during a large family reunion.	"I like trying different things and I am usually such a klutz with cooking and chemistry so it felt good to be able to do something like that."	Intellect Recognition

Events/Past Actions	Significance	Needs Met
5. George had been asked to apply for administrative positions with his school jurisdiction on several occasions although he had declined each time.	"It is always nice to be asked—and even nicer to say no and thereby maintain the illusion that you could do the job! I suppose that being asked means you are well thought of—doing a good job. And I like to think that I am."	Recognition Freedom Competition Security
6. Although he maintained that he was sorry, George remembered (with a gleam in his eye) that he had pilfered hubcaps as a teenager and was never caught.	"I was usually so damn conventional and upstanding when I was a teenager that even I began to think that I was boring. I wanted to show myself that I could do something they couldn't. So I picked the most expensive car in town and just did it. I didn't tell anybody."	Recognition Freedom Competition
7. He had stayed "successfully married" to the same woman for twenty-eight years even though many of his friends were on their second or third go-round.	"I don't think it is easy being married for a long time but it is very important to me that I have somebody who is always there for me to count on—even when I don't actually need to count on her for very much."	Security Freedom

Events/Past Actions	Significance	Needs Met
8. During college, he had toured Europe with a friend on an very sparse budget. He particularly liked seeing how far he could go with very little money and meeting new people.	"I came from a small town in the midwest and none of my family had ever been to Europe. I just felt so daring doing it. It was a real big deal back then."	Competition Freedom Adventure
9. George had been selected "Teacher of the Year" on three occasions during his career.	"I really like teaching and I think I do an excellent job at it. It felt good to have the kids give me the award—and to have everybody know that they gave it to me was the icing on the cake."	Recognition Competition Altruism
10. He had saved very scrupulously during his first fifteen years of employment and was able to completely pay for his house in record time.	"I don't like to be beholdin' to anybody, not even banks. I felt like I was finally a free man when the mortgage was finally paid off."	Security Freedom
11. During college, George had tutored a deaf student in reading skills. That student had subsequently graduated from a first-class technical institute and done very well. Twenty years later he still corresponded with George on an irregular basis.	"Tutoring David was a real challenge for me, something I had never done before. I wasn't sure that I could do it but I found I could—and I also grew to really like the boy. I don't know if I would have stuck it out if I had not really liked him."	Intellect Affiliation Altruism

Events/Past Actions	Significance	Needs Met
12. Never a great team player, George had "forced" himself to join an "old timer" basketball league comprised of teachers and their friends. To his own surprise, he had thoroughly enjoyed himself.	"I usually hate clubs and teams, a bit of a loner I guess. But, I do like individual sports and am usually pretty good at them. I don't think I would have joined on my own unless my friend had not prodded me into it. I found that I really liked it. And the cheering from the ladies didn't hurt either."	Competition Affiliation Recognition
13. While in his forties, George had maintained a secretive three-year affair with a much younger woman. Although he claimed to feel guilty about the relationship he did rate it as one of the more important events of his life.	"My wife and I were going through some pretty bad times back then. It just seemed to happen. But I remember that the talking was probably better than the sex if that makes any sense. We just seemed to drift apart the same way we had drifted together—and things at home looked better by then anyway."	Adventure Freedom Affiliation
14. George's daughter had just given birth to his first grandchild and he found that he enjoyed this new experience a great deal.	"My wife says that my granddaughter is my favorite toy and she is probably right. It just seems so awesome to think of the lineage thing and besides I get all of the fun and she still goes home to her parents at night!"	Affiliation Security

Events/Past Actions	Significance	Needs Met
15. George had done very well financially during his career, orchestrating a modest income into a substantial holding compared to that of other teachers.	"I don't really have to worry about anything financial even if I live to be a hundred and that is important to me. I still get cold shivers down my spine when I think of how poor I was during the depression or when I see a bum on the street even now."	Security Freedom Competition

It is always easier to pretend to forget the past than it is to try and squeeze some meaning from it.

RETIREMENT EXERCISE 2

Do for yourself what you have just seen done in the example of George. Using the important life experiences you wrote down earlier this chapter, identify the "Significance" of those events for you—*why* was each experience important for you? To begin with, try this for the *first two* significant events you have identified.

For each important life event you have identified ask yourself, "What is there about this event that I found especially enjoyable?" or, "Why did I identify this particular event as important?"

Once you identify *why* these events were important to you, go through the definitions of the twelve needs described in the previous chapter and write down the need(s) that were met for you by that particular experience. Be ruthlessly honest with yourself; check your initial hunches by going through the exercise a second time after you have had a chance to "sleep on" your first go-through.

If you have a trusted friend or confidant, you might want to involve that person as a validity-check to help you identify the needs indicative of your important life experiences. Do not be surprised if the needs identified by your friend do not jibe exactly with the ones you have identified. The differences might be valid but they could also be a result of your friend's inferring his or her own needs from your experiences!

You will probably find a few surprises in doing this exercise, particularly if you are able to get beyond the bland socially acceptable needs that you may be tempted to write down on your first pass through your list. Remember, by way of example, that helping someone does not necessarily reflect an Altruism need and may be more indicative of a need for Influence or Recognition.

Before you go on with your remaining examples, look at the example of Marcia, our accountant you first met earlier this chapter.

Marcia found this phase of her needs assessment difficult. "It's hard to separate why I thought the event was important when I did it from why I think it is important now," she noted. However, she did produce the following list based on her best estimation of why the events were important to her.

Events/Past Actions	Significance	Needs Met
1. Although she had worked full time for only three years before quitting to have children, Marcia was especially proud that her firm had thought enough of her performance to offer her another full-time position nine years later, once her children had reached school age.	"I had never thought that I was extraordinarily good at anything before I went to work. But, I quickly found out that I could out-perform many of the more senior employees— including the men. It felt good to be in a situation where it was okay to compete and to do well and it just reinforced things when I was re- membered enough to be offered another job when I went back to work after having my children."	Recognition Competition

Events/Past Actions	**Significance**	**Needs Met**
2. Marcia was an accomplished musician and had played the bassoon with her local symphony for many years. She enjoyed the challenge of playing with younger people, some of whom were professional musicians, and she remembered with pride the twenty-five-year service plaque that had been presented to her at the conclusion of the previous year's season.	"I just love music. It is so ordered and so beautiful at the same time. I especially enjoy working with the young musicians just starting out with the symphony. They're so much better than I was when I was their age— and so much fun to teach and work with. I remember how honored I felt when I stood up to receive my service plaque. The applause from the audience nearly lifted me out of the auditorium."	Affiliation Aesthetics Recognition Adventure
3. During her "dating years," Marcia had been very popular as well as strikingly beautiful. She indicated that this had been very important for her at the time and was remembered with much fondness many years later.	"I always felt sort of homely when I was a teenager and in my early twenties. It surprised me that men were interested in me more so than my older sister whom I had always thought of as more beautiful and smarter. I used to spend hours 'looking beautiful' even when I was not particularly interested in the men I was looking beautiful for."	Recognition Adventure Competition

Events/Past Actions	Significance	Needs Met
4. Marcia had been very active with a local voluntary organization that dealt with girls without mothers. She particularly enjoyed her work extending over a seven-year term with a troubled adolescent who had progressed to a much less troubled young woman.	"My relationship with my mother was not a particularly happy one so I thought it would be important to help girls who had even a worse relationship—or none at all—with their mothers. My work with Janice was particularly important because she 'turned out all right' and I can say that I had a big part to play in that."	Influence Affiliation Altruism
5. For a period of five years, Marcia had taught an evening accounting class for her local community college and had enjoyed it very much.	"I really enjoyed teaching even though I was scared stiff the first time I did it. I was so used to worrying that I didn't know anything that it felt good to be thought of as knowing everything! Besides, it paid well for the little time it took."	Recognition Influence Materialism
6. Marcia was the financial manager for the investments of her husband and herself. Although a very conservative individual, she was very consistent and enduring, building a sizeable "nest egg" over a thirty-year period. She looked on this with a good deal of pride.	"Although I probably wouldn't tell him that, my husband knows nothing about finances. In the first few years that we were married he handled everything and really botched it up. I took over more-or-less out of necessity and have done very well. Financially, we're pretty good now and that makes everything a lot easier—particularly the worrying."	Competition Recognition Freedom Security

Events/Past Actions	Significance	Needs Met
7. Marcia had enjoyed her children very much. She especially remembered two events: the marriage of her eldest daughter and the graduation from high school of her son, who was not a good student.	"When I was married, having children was something you took pretty much for granted. But I found that I really enjoyed them—still do. They seem to tie things together for me, make it more of a family than a collection of like-minded individuals."	Security Affiliation Aesthetics
8. Marcia's husband was an avid fisherman and she accompanied him on many of his weekend and holiday trips. Although she was only modestly interested in fishing at the beginning, this interest had grown over the years. As well, she noted that "it's hard to avoid talking to each other when you're sitting together in the middle of a lake."	"Let's get one thing straight. I'm still not all that enamored with fishing and I probably would not do it if Fred (husband) didn't. But I occasionally get a kick out of getting a much bigger fish than he did and it does force us to talk—something we both agree is important but don't do enough of."	Affiliation Security Competition
9. Marcia had been active in politics at the local level. She particularly enjoyed her involvement as the treasurer and executive member of the campaign committee for a successful mayoralty candidate in her home town.	"I got into politics through the back door, not out of any particular political convictions. I knew the mayorality candidate socially and got involved that way. But I really enjoyed the planning and intrigue you go through in a campaign	Affiliation Intellect Recognition

Events/Past Actions	Significance	Needs Met
	and I got a chance to manage the finances from the ground up, something I don't get to do with my multinational oil company."	
10. Marcia had gone through some "emotional problems" when she was in her early fifties and reported that her involvement with her church and a self-help group associated with her church was instrumental in her improvement.	"Religion was always in the background of my life but it was never something I was fanatical about. I did find it very soothing, probably more so because my husband and I were going through a rough period at that point in time."	Religion Security
11. Marcia had been present at the deaths of both her father and mother, and although it had been upsetting, she regarded these as very important points in her life.	"I was not particularly close to my parents and I don't know why it seems important that I was there when they died. Maybe it is because I want my children to be there when it is my turn."	Affiliation Religion
12. During high school, Marcia had been very active (and effective) at public speaking, an area she regretted not being more involved in during her later life.	"There is something powerful about standing up in front of a group of people and having them listen to you. I was scared but it was incredibly exhilarating. I don't know why I stopped doing that."	Recognition Adventure Competition

Events/Past Actions	Significance	Needs Met
13. Over the course of her long career with the oil company, Marcia had been involved in several large-scale system changes, including two different computerizations. She had enjoyed these substantial disruptions although they were very demanding when they occurred.	"Sometimes work gets pretty routine and there is a certain kind of security about that—even though it is boring. The system changes were very complex, particularly one of them. But I really enjoyed them because they put your brains back to work. It was like learning another language."	Intellect Recognition
14. While in their late forties, Marcia and her husband had designed and built their own home. Although, at the time, the project had nearly driven them both crazy, Marcia was proud of what they had done together—and with the result.	"I had always wanted to design a house from scratch. Over the years I probably paid enough in house renovation and housebuilding books and magazines to pay for a new house so it was good to finally do it! It drove my husband and I apart and pulled us back together and it was probably the most creative thing I have ever done. I loved it and I hated it."	Aesthetics Security Recognition Adventure
15. Marcia was one of the first women employed by her oil-company employer to be promoted to a middle management position. She was very proud of this.	"Management was something you never thought much about when you were a woman working in a man's world. I knew I was better than many of my bosses and it felt good when they finally	Recognition Competition Influence

Events/Past Actions	Significance	Needs Met
	realized the same thing. Looking back, I probably should have been more aggressive about it and it probably would have happened earlier."	

RETIREMENT EXERCISE 2—*continued*

Finish the analysis you have already started of your important life experiences. Keep in mind that you must progress from deciding *why* the event was important to you to deciding the *needs* that each experience met for you.

"Averaging Across" the Needs Met by Your Life Experiences

By now, you have either identified a good number of needs met by a sample of your individual life experiences or you have pulled out your hair in trying to do so. If you are in the second category, take a two- or three-day break from all of this self-analysis and try again later. This next step is for those of you who have already identified a number of important needs in your life.

You have probably noticed a number of similarities as well as a good number of dissimilarities in the needs you have identified for each important life event. Some needs will have been mentioned many times, others very seldom or not at all. We can see that this is true of George and Marcia, the two individuals whose experiences we have been tracking through the earlier examples. Here is what we find simply by counting the number of times each need is cited in the "Needs Met" column for each of them.

Need	George	Marcia
Influence	2	3
Altruism	2	1
Affiliation	6	6
Competition	7	6
Intellect	3	2
Aesthetics	0	3
Security	5	5
Recognition	8	10
Adventure	3	4
Freedom	7	1
Materialism	0	1
Religion	0	2

It is easy to see that George's main needs are Recognition, Competition, Freedom, and Affiliation. Security is a strong need too; it appears five times in his list of fifteen events. On the other hand, Aesthetics, Materialism, and Religion are not mentioned once.

For Marcia, in contrast, a single need stands out dramatically. While Affiliation, Competition, and Security are all strong, they are overshadowed by Recognition, mentioned ten times.

RETIREMENT EXERCISE 3

Do this exercise based on your own needs you have identified in Exercise 2. Count the number of times each need appears in your "Needs Met" column and compile a list for yourself, as was done for George and Marcia. Keep in mind that your profile would only be completely accurate if you could identify *all* of your important life experiences and also have some way to quantify the importance of each experience in a relative way. However, this profile will give you an excellent starting point, and even in cases where more exhaustive needs identification is undertaken, this method holds its own in terms of overall accuracy. As with most methods, the accuracy increases (together with the requisite effort!) in direct proportion to the number of important experiences you are able to identify.

A word of caution. Although it is often attempted, it is difficult to do the exercises in this chapter in reverse, that is, going from the definitions of various needs to identifying past experiences that are indicative of these needs. This is because most of us are cheaters at heart—perhaps not consciously but cheaters none the less! It is too easy to be selective in identifying only those experiences indicative of the needs you think you have rather than starting from your experiences and inferring your needs from these experiences.

There are several evident themes that run across the examples of George and Marcia you have seen in this chapter. In each case, there are certain things that each has tried to glean from life thus far. These strivings cut across all "seasons" of their lives, from early adulthood to maturity. Their strivings will not end with their retirement just as your strivings will not end with your retirement.

We will now turn from your past strivings to your future wishes, in order to learn what they can tell you about your life-long needs.

Chapter 4

Other Ways
to Identify
Your Needs

"Dream, dream, for this is also sooth."
—William Butler Yeats,
"The Song of the Happy Shepherd"

Like your past life experiences, your wishes for the future are important in retirement planning, not for what they are per se, but for the needs these wishes represent. In reflecting on your past, you will know that there have been many things you might have wanted to do in years gone by that have proved impossible for you. You might have been too unintelligent, too poor, too busy, or too proud to take advantage of these opportunities. This did not mean that the needs those opportunities could have met for you were doomed to remain unsatisfied forever. You accommodated. You found other opportunities. You met your needs by other, more possible means.

In the same way it has been in your past, any particular wish you might have for the future may prove impossible to realize. You might still be too unintelligent, too poor, too busy, or too proud to bring these wishes to fruition. Luckily, your capacity to meet your needs is not dependent on your ability to pursue any *single* course of action—there will always be alternatives in your future as there have always been alternatives in your past and your challenge will be to find them.

For many years, career and retirement planners focused solely on the future to help their clients plan for the future. The typical procedure used in such approaches was to have individuals identify what they wanted out of the next five, ten, or fifteen years—their dreams—and then develop a lock-step procedure to get them there. Unfortunately this approach often worked much better in theory than it did in practice.

The biggest problem in basing your retirement decisions *solely* on your future projected wishes is that such decision-making often leads to selecting future courses of action that are based on your *greatest unmet needs at the present time* rather than a balance of important needs that are being met in your present life circumstances as well as those that are not being met. This is because your wishes are a much better indicator of your needs that are *not* being met right now rather than an indicator of your needs "on average." In basing retirement decisions solely on your wishes, the driving power of your unmet needs would be too strong in relation to the motivating power of your needs that are being satisfied at present. Your current situation would cloud your thinking and result in your making retirement decisions with long-term implications on the basis of transitory feelings.

After all, there would be little doubt as to your actual decision if you were to decide between eating and reading a good book when you were famished. Yet that is exactly the same principle operating in an exclusively future-oriented planning method. The exclusive use of your wishes in planning for your retirement leads to a bias, a bias that could prove dangerous if used as your *sole* guide to your future.

With this caveat in mind, it is still possible to use your future wishes as a *supplement* to the more reliable past-oriented information we have already looked at in planning for your retirement. Firstly, when you isolate what your wishes tell you about yourself and compare this to what you have identified by analyzing your past, you get a good indication of longer-term needs that are *not being met in your present life circumstances*. Secondly, if the information obtained by analyzing such wishes is considerably different from that obtained by the analysis of your past, it indicates that you are either not very happy with your *present* life circumstances or have wishes that are closer to what my mother used to call "pipe dreams." In either case—act with caution in using exclusively your wishes for your retirement planning!

Your Dreams and Aspirations

Now that I have convinced you of the folly in using your wishes in your future planning, let us look at how these wishes and dreams can be used to supplement the more rigorous past-oriented information you have already collected. The process is simple even if interpreting the results is not!

In using your dreams and aspirations as a supplement to identifying your needs it is important to remember that they are just that—dreams and aspirations! As such, they are not hemmed in by concerns about practicality or "do-ability." They reflect desires that, even when they are totally impractical or impossible, can tell you something about your needs—something that can eventually lead you to creative and alternate ways to satisfaction. You probably will not be able to realize all your dreams, but taking a close look at them makes it much more likely that you will understand your needs more clearly and be able to satisfy these needs in one way or another.

Here are some examples of the dreams and aspirations identified by Terry, a soon-to-be-retired senior geologist employed by a regional oil exploration firm.

1. "I want to get a pilot's license and fly across the country on a long extended holiday. I have always wanted to do that. I don't know why I didn't get my license years ago."
2. "I came from a farming background and I have always wanted to do some farming. I have been thinking of selling-out in the city and buying a hobby farm a short distance from town."
3. "I have always thought it would be nice just to do nothing for a while—read, think, grow moss on the soles of my feet! But what if I didn't like it?"

4. "You know, this will sound silly but I would like to pan for gold. Over the years I have been cataloging some likely spots and maybe I should do something about them now that I have the time."

5. "I know that some of my older colleagues did some part-time consulting in geology after they retired—some of them for my own company. Maybe I could do that for a while."

6. "I have grandchildren spread right across the country and I want to spend more time with them. I want to see more of my own kids now that they're old enough to know what it's all about."

7. "When I was going to college way back when, I took a degree in geology but I did take one course in drama and really enjoyed it. I even acted in a few plays during college. I sometimes think about going back to university to study things that are enjoyable rather than what you have to."

8. "I have always been a hunter and a fisherman but I've never really gone on an elaborate trip, the kind you read about in *Outdoor Life*. I'd like to go to one of those fly-in camps way up in British Columbia."

9. "I used to be quite an artist when I was a teenager, even did some semicommercial work during the summer when I was at college. Maybe I would like to paint although I've probably forgotten how to do it now."

10. "I've always been a gardener, particularly flowers. For years I've talked of building an add-on greenhouse at the house. Maybe I should do it now."

RETIREMENT EXERCISE 4

Write down two of your own dreams or aspirations. Remember that they need not be practical, realizable, or concerned with satisfying anybody except yourself.

Here are other examples of wishes and aspirations, this time from Lorraine, a researcher employed by a large university medical laboratory. Lorraine had six months of service left before retirement.

1. "I have always liked photography. Not the kind of technical photography I've had to use in my work—the real kind that's only done because you like it. I have always wanted to publish a book on wildlife photography, something that would make people sit up and take notice."

2. "I think I would like to spend some real time with my granddaughter and grandson. When I raised my own two daughters I was always too busy to enjoy them. They don't live in the same city and I don't want to move but perhaps something could be worked out."

3. "I have always wanted to start my own business—high-quality tailored clothes for women. But I don't want to be tied down to a business so I don't really know what I want."

4. "Now that I can afford it, I want to travel. Not so much to the usual tourist haunts—more the out-of-the-way places that most people never get to."

5. "I've been a tennis player for more years than I care to remember. Just once I would love to go to Wimbledon."

6. "My husband died five years ago. I keep thinking about the good times we had together (as well as the bad) and I would like that again with somebody else if I could."

7. "With my husband's life insurance, pension, and my own savings and pension, I'm pretty well off financially but I want to learn more about investing and managing money. I always have the feeling that others—accountant, broker, etc.—don't really care about my money as much as I do."

8. "I feel like I really haven't left my mark and I'd still like to do something that would do that. Probably something in writing or music although I'm only a decided amateur in both of them."

9. "It sounds crazy but I would still like to build the retirement home on my lake property that my husband and I had talked about and planned for years."

10. "I've been on the board of our local symphony for some time now. I would really like to be the chairwoman but I don't know how to go about doing it."

RETIREMENT EXERCISE 4—*continued*

Try to identify and write down other examples of future-oriented activities that you think would be meaningful for you. As you did in identifying past activities that were important to you, be careful to identify active and specific wishes rather than vague assertions, such as "I want to be happy."

In rare cases, individuals are unable to identify any concrete wishes for the future. They do not feel driven to do anything. This situation arises from one of two reasons, total satisfaction or total dissatisfaction. In the first instance, the individual is unable to identify wishes because his or her current life circumstances allow for the meeting of all needs and there is very little driving or motivational power in met needs. In the second instance, the individual has no wishes because his or her needs are quite unmet, have been so for a considerable time, and this has resulted in depression and giving-up—the "I don't want what I cannot have" syndrome. Both of these instances are unusual, and even where they do occur, the individual will still need to contend with the altered life circumstances brought about by retirement. In such cases, a sole source of data must be used—meaningful past actions.

Making Sense Out of Your Future Wishes

The same procedure you used to unearth the hidden meaning in your past life experiences can be applied to your wishes and aspirations. In the case of your wishes, the process involves asking yourself "What is there about this example that I think I would find meaningful or important?" or "Why do I want to do this?" From there you go on to develop your hunches of the needs represented by your examples in much the same way as you already did for your past activities.

By way of example I will follow up with Terry, our retiring geologist from earlier in this chapter.

Events/Future Wishes	Significance	Needs Represented
1. "I want to get a pilot's license and fly across the country on a long extended holiday. I have always wanted to do that. I don't know why I didn't get my license years ago."	"I've always had to fly in small planes a lot as part of my work and in some ways I've always envied the pilots. I mean you can go anywhere, do anything you want. You're alone when you want to be and nothing can bother you when you are up there."	Freedom Aesthetics
2. "I came from a farming background and I have always wanted to do some farming. I have been thinking of selling-out in the city and buying a hobby farm a short distance from town."	"The more I've worked at other things, the more I know why my father loved farming. You are your own boss and you have the freedom to go bankrupt without anybody telling you how! Besides, nothing smells like a farm in the spring."	Freedom Affiliation Security Aesthetics

Events/Future Wishes	Significance	Needs Repre- sented
3. "I have always thought it would be nice just to do nothing for a while—read, think, grow moss on the soles of my feet! But what if I didn't like it?"	"My work has always been hectic. Just when you think you've got everything under control, some regulation or another changes. I like it but it also drives me crazy sometimes. I think a rest would be nice."	Freedom Security
4. "You know, this will sound silly but I would like to pan for gold. Over the years I have been cataloging some likely spots and maybe I should do something about them now that I will have the time."	"There have always been small finds made this way. I have given away a number to friends over the years. Besides that's really the part of geology I like, basic prospecting. Not this damned management non-sense that takes forever to get a decision."	Freedom Competition Adventure
5. "I think that some of my older colleagues did some part-time consulting in geology after they re-tired—some of them for my own company. Maybe I could do that for a while."	"I am pretty certain I can survive off my pension and other financial inter-ests but the extra money would be nice. Besides, I am not sure if I can just stop like that. The work might drive me crazy sometimes but all-in-all it's still pretty good."	Materialism Security Affiliation

Events/Future Wishes	Significance	Needs Represented
6. "I have grandchildren spread right across the country and I want to spend more time with them. I want to see more of my own kids now that they're old enough to know what it's all about."	"When my kids were growing up it seems like I was always out of town on some site or another. I know it's too late to start over but I really enjoy the kids. They really should get to know their grandpa."	Affiliation Security
7. "When I was going to college way back when, I took a degree in geology but I did take one course in drama and really enjoyed it. I even acted in a few plays during college. I sometimes think about going back to university to study things that are enjoyable rather than what you have to."	"I think I've done just about as much as I want to with geology. Rocks and oil are still interesting but I'm more interested in people just now. I've always been a reader and I think it might be fun to study something different now that I don't have to worry about passing."	Affiliation Intellect
8. "I have always been a hunter and a fisherman but I've never really gone on an elaborate trip, the kind you read about in *Outdoor Life*. I'd like to go to one of those fly-in camps way up in British Columbia."	"To me, hunting and fishing are the best parts of my work, the chance to get away from it all in the most beautiful parts of the country. Besides, I would really like to get a trophy, something that would be outstanding."	Aesthetics Competition

Events/Future Wishes	Significance	Needs Repre-sented
9. "I used to be quite an artist when I was a teenager, even did some semicommercial work during the summer when I was at college. Maybe I would like to paint although I've probably forgotten how to do it now."	"I don't know if I could really do anything that would be very good any more. Maybe I just remember that I was better at it than I am! I need something that will push me, something that has no bounds."	Aesthetics Competition Intellect
10. "I've always been a gardener, particularly flowers. For years I've talked of building an add-on greenhouse at the house. Maybe I should do it now."	"I think I might enjoy designing and building it more than I would enjoy using it. I've got some novel ideas for heating and cooling the system that could tie in with my house. Besides, my wife likes gardening too."	Intellect Affiliation

RETIREMENT EXERCISE 5

It is time for you to attempt this exercise for yourself. Try it initially for the first two wishes or aspirations you identified earlier in this chapter. Remember to start by identifying why the wish is important to you and only then try to identify the needs represented by those wishes.

By way of further example, here is Lorraine's assessment of the needs identified through an analysis of her wishes and aspirations.

Events/Future Wishes	Significance	Needs Represented
1. "I have always liked photography. Not the kind of technical photography I've had to use in my work—the real kind that's only done because you like it. I have always wanted to publish a book on wildlife photography, something that would make people sit up and take notice."	"Originally, when I started using photography in my work, I really enjoyed it. Later, it got to be a boring technical chore. But I do like what you can do with photography once you have all the technical things mastered—especially when you don't have to do it. I like doing things outdoors and this would give me some focus to what I do."	Aesthetics Freedom Adventure
2. "I think I would like to spend some real time with my granddaughter and grandson. When I raised my own two daughters I was always too busy to enjoy them. They don't live in the same city and I don't want to move but perhaps something could be worked out."	"I started working at a time when it was not usual or popular for women to do so. In some ways, I felt guilty about doing it. Maybe I want to substitute my grandchildren for my own kids, I don't know. I do enjoy being around them, and my daughters seem to enjoy it when I am there as well."	Security Affiliation Influence
3. "I have always wanted to start my own business—high-quality tailored clothes for women. But I don't want to be tied	"I have always worked *for* someone, and while I've enjoyed it, I often thought I could do a better job of running things	Freedom Aesthetics Competition

Events/Future Wishes	Significance	Needs Repre- sented
down to a business so I don't really know what I want."	myself. I would want it to be something 'artsy' and small enough so that I could do nearly every-thing myself or using only part-time help."	
4. "Now that I can afford it, I want to travel. Not so much to the usual tourist haunts—more the out-of-the-way places that most people never get to."	"I've always liked to do things out of the ordinary, I don't know why. I love to know things, to have seen things that are un-common. A bit of a show-off I guess."	Recognition Competition Adventure Freedom
5. "I've been a tennis player for more years than I care to remember. Just once I would love to go to Wimbledon."	"During Wimbledon I watch more television than I do throughout the rest of the year. It's excit-ing and it is almost like an exclusive cult."	Recognition Adventure Competition
6. "My husband died five years ago. I keep thinking about the good times we had together (as well as the bad) and I would like that again with somebody else if I could."	"I suspect it's just an idle wish at my age. I'm not sure I know how to start. Besides, it took my hus-band and me our first ten years to get used to each other and I haven't got time for that again!"	Security Affiliation
7. "With my husband's life insurance, pension, and my own savings and pension, I'm pretty well	"I don't really like being dependent on other peo-ple, even when I am pay-ing them to do it. It can't	Freedom Intellect Security

Events/Future Wishes	Significance	Needs Represented
off financially but I want to learn more about investing and managing money. I always have the feeling that others—accountant, broker, etc.—don't really care about my money as much as I do."	possibly be any more difficult than my field, and besides, it would be fun to learn something different."	
8. "I feel like I really haven't left my mark and I'd still like to do something that would do that. Probably something in writing or music although I'm only a decided amateur in both of them."	"I know it is natural to feel like 'time is running out' but I think I have always felt this way. Maybe it's because everything you're doing seems important at the time you are doing it but less so in hindsight. I know I am never going to win a Nobel prize but I would like to leave something."	Competition Recognition
9. "It sounds crazy but I would still like to build the retirement home on my lake property that my husband and I had talked about and planned for years."	"It just seems like unfinished business, something that needs to be done for things to be right. I know it is foolish and I wouldn't want to live there alone but something inside me keeps thinking about it."	Affiliation Altruism

Events/Future Wishes	Significance	Needs Repre- sented
10. "I've been on the board of our local symphony for some time now. I would really like to be the chairwoman but I don't know how to go about doing it."	"For years, I've listened to men who knew far less than I do tell me how to run a symphony. It seems like such an 'old boys club.' I think I understand how to do the job, especially about how to get the board working together and it would be fun to try out my ideas."	Recognition Intellect Competition

RETIREMENT EXERCISE 5—*continued*

Complete this exercise for your other wishes and aspirations. Pay particular attention to the *Needs* you think you are manifesting by your dreams.

RETIREMENT EXERCISE 6

Once you have identified the needs that are represented by your wishes and dreams, count how many times each need is cited as being important for you.

Wishes Change—Needs Endure

It is one thing to hear that your wishes are merely representations of unmet needs—needs that could probably be met through other activities. It is quite another to believe that anything could ever take the place of your long-standing dream to relocate in northern Brazil!

Throughout our lives, most of us have felt driven by our wishes, by things we would like to do. In some cases, we have been able to realize these wishes and been satisfied. In other circumstances, internal or external circumstances have prevented us from doing so. In cases where we have been unsuccessful, we are unsatisfied, perhaps feel sad or disappointed. After a period of mourning we usually accommodate our feelings by pursuing other wishes. This type of substitution is a naturally occurring process but it is one that is usually entered into unknowingly. We are unknowing because we enter the process by pursuing wishes without a conscious knowledge of the needs such wishes represent for us. We see our wishes as a product rather than as a process that can lead to a product, that product being the reduction in the driving power of our needs.

Your wishes will come and go, although they may be compelling, even overwhelming, at times. Your needs will not change although your success at fulfilling your wishes will change the relative perceived strengths of your needs at any given time. If you are lucky in fulfilling your wishes the needs represented by these wishes will reduce in intensity but you will find yourself pursuing other wishes, wishes that either represent different needs or further satisfaction of your original needs.

If you do not understand your needs you are a victim of the unknowing processes that move you from wish to wish, sometimes being satisfied when the wish is fulfilled, sometimes not. If you understand your needs, you will be able to understand why some wishes were meaningful when they were fulfilled whereas others were not. But more importantly, you will have a focal point to develop and evaluate new wishes. You will be able to evaluate how useful a proposed course of action will be for you without actually pursuing that course of action. You acquire this ability not by understanding your wishes but by understanding your needs. In retirement terms, this is using your past to plan your future.

Chapter 5

Pulling It All Together

"A long pull, and a strong pull, and a pull all together."
—Charles Dickens, *David Copperfield*

The first step in using your needs to plan your retirement future is to compare the needs you have identified by examining your past actions and those identified through your future wishes. Don't expect the needs identified by the two methods to be exactly the same—a highly rated need compiled from your list of past actions might have somewhat less priority on your list of needs compiled from your future wishes. For example, you might find that Recognition is near the top of the list of needs identified from your past actions but that it is somewhat less important as identified from your future wishes.

In fact, if a need is very strong as identified by analyzing your past actions it might not even appear on your list of needs identified by analyzing your wishes. There is a simple reason for this in that if a need is being fully satisfied in your current life, that need lacks the driving force to be represented in your wishes. It is the same logic that makes you poorly motivated to worry about dinner immediately after satisfying yourself at lunch! This does not mean that such a need is unimportant. Quite the reverse, it means that satisfaction of this need will require special attention when retirement changes your current life circumstances in a way that alters the opportunities available to you to meet your needs.

Examples Revisited

Let us return to the examples provided by Terry (geologist) and Lorraine (medical researcher) profiled in the previous chapter. In each case, their most highly rated needs, as identified by their past actions and future wishes, are at the top of the list.

Terry's Lists of Needs

Past Actions	Future Wishes
Intellect	Affiliation
Competition	Freedom
Recognition	Aesthetics
Materialism	Security
Influence	Competition
Adventure	Intellect
Security	Materialism
	Adventure

Keep in mind that, although each list is presented in a priority order, there may be very little difference between the strength of needs that are one or two steps removed from each other on the list. This is because of the usual errors that are present in any measuring scheme such as this and the fact that we have identified only a sample of Terry's past actions and wishes rather than a comprehensive list. But, although it is not a perfect measurement, it is still useful.

The differences between Terry's lists illustrate the similarities and differences you should expect in assimilating the information you have compiled from the different sources. In Terry's case, the differences between his two lists are largely explainable from differences between his current life situation and his long-term life "average" situation.

For example, Intellect and Influence needs are being very well met in Terry's current work and nonwork life and therefore assume less priority in his wishes for the future, not because these needs are not important, but because they lack a driving or motivating force for him at present. It is not likely that you wish for what you already have.

On the other hand, although Affiliation, Freedom, and Aesthetics are highly placed in "Future Wishes," they do not appear on the other list. These are good examples of less important needs assuming first-order significance in Terry's future wishes because the minimal opportunities for their satisfaction in his current life results in a heightened driving power for these needs. Without the more balanced view afforded by the analysis of his meaningful past actions, Terry might attach undue importance to such wishes in planning for his future.

Lorraine's Lists of Needs

Past Actions	Future Wishes
Intellect	Competition
Security	Freedom
Competition	Recognition
Recognition	Security
Aesthetics	Adventure
Materialism	Affiliation
Altruism	Aesthetics
	Intellect

Although the needs identified by Lorraine are different in some ways from those of Terry, her case demonstrates many of the same principles. Once again, Intellect is prominent on the basis of the first list but is low on the list derived from future wishes. This is explainable from Lorraine's current life circumstances that allow for rich opportunities to meet this need. Freedom and Adventure demonstrate the reverse situation, again attributable to a current life situation that is very staid and conservative. Competition is prominent in both lists suggesting that it is both strong and somewhat less satisfied than Lorraine would like in her life at the present time.

RETIREMENT EXERCISE 7

Using a fresh sheet of paper, list the needs you have identified through analyzing your past actions and future wishes in Exercises 3 and 6. Put the needs on these two lists in order of priority, with the needs mentioned the most times at the top of each list.

Interpreting Your Needs Assessment Data

Like Terry and Lorraine, when you compare the needs you have identified by analyzing your wishes and aspirations with those you previously identified by analyzing your past activities you will probably notice some similarities—and some differences as well. There are several possible reasons for these similarities and differences, reasons that have to do with how similar your current opportunities for needs satisfaction are to the "average opportunity level" that has characterized your life up to the present. You may be in a better, worse, or average position with regards to the present opportunities available to you to meet your needs than has been usual for you over the longer term.

Here are some guidelines for the interpretation of your results based on differences between the needs you identified from your wishes and those you identified from your past actions.

1. If the needs identified by analyzing your future wishes are very different in kind from the needs identified through your analysis of your meaningful past experiences, be cautious in putting much stock in the needs identified through your wishes. Although it is difficult, you must avoid being unduly swayed in your decision-making by driving forces or needs that appear

prominent in your current situation but which your evidence indicates are not apparent in your past. The only case where this caveat would not apply is where life's circumstances have totally prevented you from meeting certain of your needs throughout your life. In the vast majority of cases, if you have a genuine need, you will have done *something* to reduce the intensity of that need throughout your life. And you will have remembered that something.

2. If the needs identified by analyzing your future wishes are *exactly the same* as the needs identified by analyzing your meaningful past experiences, it is likely that you now are at the point in your life where the current opportunities available to you to meet your needs are *less than* the long-run average of such opportunities throughout your life. This means that you are currently striving to meet genuine needs of long-standing duration for which you do not have current opportunities for satisfaction. This is a healthy state to be in and is analgous to being hungry enough to seek food (and thereby avoid starvation!). If you are in this position, you will need to give particular attention to creating new opportunities for yourself. (More on this topic later).

3. If the needs identified by analyzing your future wishes are somewhat different, more in degree than kind, from the needs identified by analyzing your meaningful past experiences, note carefully *the direction* of these differences. If the needs appear stronger as evidenced from your wishes, it is likely that the needs identified from your wishes represent genuine needs that, while you have been able to satisfy them to some degree throughout your life, remain unsatisfied at present. Conversely, if the needs appear stronger as evidenced from your past actions rather than your wishes, it is likely that your current situation is better than your long-term circumstances in providing you opportunities to meet these needs. In either case you have useful information to use in evaluating your future prospects.

Deciding on Your Needs

Having read this far, you know the importance of identifying your genuine long-term needs. These are the needs that you must seek to satisfy in the altered life circumstances that will characterize your retirement. In evaluating opportunities that come your way or in creating opportunities, these long-term needs will provide you with the guidance you need to make competent decisions. Keep in mind that these needs are important and should be used in your decision-making about your future even if such needs are not being met in your present life circumstances. You can have a future that is better than your present—but you must plan for it.

Now that you have listed the needs identified through analyzing your past actions and future wishes, you can complete the process of putting it all together. In some cases, where the needs identified through both methods are the same, this is comparatively easy. But for most people, this is not the case and some difficult decisions must be made. Before you try the process yourself, look at the examples for Terry and Lorraine.

Terry's Lists of Needs

Past Actions	Future Wishes	Long-term Needs
Intellect	Affiliation	Intellect
Competition	Freedom	Competition
Recognition	Aesthetics	Recognition
Materialism	Security	Materialism
Influence	Competition	Adventure
Adventure	Intellect	Security
Security	Materialism	Affiliation
	Adventure	Aesthetics

Lorraine's Lists of Needs

Past Actions	Future Wishes	Long-term Needs
Intellect	Competition	Security
Security	Freedom	Competition
Competition	Recognition	Intellect
Recognition	Security	Recognition
Aesthetics	Adventure	Aesthetics
Materialism	Affiliation	Adventure
Altruism	Aesthetics	Materialism
	Intellect	Altruism
		Aesthetics
		Affiliation

Both Terry and Lorraine expressed some degree of surprise at their final lists of long-term needs. Like most of us, they were much more aware of their immediate needs, needs that were not being met in their present life circumstances, than they were of "the bigger picture." For each of them, if decisions had been made solely on the basis of their more pressing immediate concerns, important decisions about their future could have been seriously flawed.

The process of completing the third column, "Long-term Needs," is very much an individual matter and therefore difficult to document in any "how-to" sense. Based on the points already outlined in this chapter, here are some general guidelines to help you:

1. As already noted at earlier stages of this process, put most of the weight on needs established by analyzing your past actions. In cases such as Terry's and Lorraine's where you find a need represented both in past actions and future wishes, this is good evidence to include it nearer the top of your final list of long-term needs. The priority for such needs is usually closer to the one established through analyzing past actions than future wishes.

2. If you find a need represented in your analysis of your past actions but not represented in your analysis of your future

wishes, do not ignore it. It is likely that, although this need is significant, it is being sufficiently well met in your present life circumstances. As your life circumstances change with retirement, such a need will exert renewed driving force. The ranking for such a need on your list of long-term needs, although perhaps slightly lower than the ranking on your list of needs identified through analyzing your past actions, will still be close to that level of importance.

3. If you find a need represented in your list of needs identified through analyzing your future wishes but absent or very low in priority on your list of needs established through analyzing your past actions, act cautiously in including such needs very far up in priority in your list of long-term needs. It is likely that, relatively speaking, such needs are really quite low in priority but that they are not being met at all in your present life circumstances.

4. Do not become overly concerned with the priority ranking to the extent of worrying whether or not a particular need should be ranked first, second, or third. Although it is possible to distinguish quite clearly between needs placed at the bottom and the top of your ranked lists, needs that are similar in strength make it very difficult to make such refined distinctions. Besides, there is little reason to do so since you will need to develop a plan to satisfy all similarily ranked needs.

RETIREMENT EXERCISE 8

In the same manner as the examples of Terry and Lorraine, it is time for you to compile your own final list of needs, to summarize the results from the exercises you have completed so far. Do not be concerned if you cannot make a clear distinction between a first-ranked and a second-ranked need. It is only important that you are able to identify your most important needs as higher in priority than your other needs.

Incompatible Needs

Once you have identified your stable long-term needs, you are ready to take a closer look at your long-term needs that appear to be incompatible or mutually exclusive. You might find that you have identified Security and Adventure as very important or there may be other needs you think cannot both be satisfied in a single life. Sometimes, as in the examples we have already seen, these apparent differences are due largely to the differences between the opportunities available to you in your present life circumstances and the opportunities available to you "on average" throughout your life. In such cases, these are not inconsistencies in your needs but rather in opportunities to meet your needs. However, many apparent inconsistencies are genuine. You may genuinely need to satisfy a Security and Adventure need in your life in order to be satisfied.

In the case where the inconsistencies reflect the real you, it is seldom possible to resolve them if resolve means *deciding between* meeting need one or another. Rather, resolution should be thought of in terms of *understanding* the differences, the relative importance of the needs that appear to be in conflict, and how the satisfaction of such needs can be accommodated within a single life.

To be realistic, you should expect apparent inconsistencies in your needs because they reflect the diversity that is you. It is normal for adults to have inconsistent, even incompatible needs. Typically, you do not need to satisfy a need for Security *or* Adventure but rather Security *and* Adventure. Rather than pretend you do not have one or another of such needs—a sure bet for psychological unhappiness—the trick is to achieve some sort of *balance* in meeting both needs in your day-to-day life. Besides, with incompatible needs, it is likely that both are not top priority and it will be possible to organize your life in such a manner to achieve a "best fit" in meeting both.

Needs that are apparently incompatible represent the biggest challenge to your ability to develop personal action plans—to select and pursue opportunities—based on your needs. Frequently, the folly is in thinking that every single action you undertake must be in agreement with all of your needs. This is seldom possible, and most times you will need to do a number of different things in order to meet different needs. You will need to respond appropriately to a variety of opportunities, opportunities that may seem to pull you in several directions at the same time.

Satisfying your needs means that your retirement, like all of your life before retirement, must be governed by variety in order to be satisfying. But it must be a chosen variety, a variety that provides you with the opportunities you will require to meet your needs. It is identifying those needs now met primarily by your work that we will look at in the next section. Because, once you know what you need, you are in the best position to capitalize on life's circumstances—opportunities—to get it.

Chapter 6

Your Needs and Your Current Circumstances

"The present contains nothing more than the past,
and what is found in the effect was already in the cause."
—Henri Bergson, *Creative Evolution*

There are two "laws" that are important to remember in using your needs assessment information in planning for your retirement. The first law is that your needs will not change when you retire—even though the opportunities to meet your needs might change drastically. The second law is that there are always ways, other than those in which you are currently engaged, to meet your needs.

Ignoring the first law can result in great unhappiness because nothing is done to plan for or deal with the loss of the opportunities to meet your needs that are provided by your present work or life circumstances. Ignoring the second law results in restricting yourself to seeking a retirement that is as close as possible—in terms of actual activity—to your work life, or, more likely, results in stubbornly refusing to retire until ill health or work pressures force a hurried and unplanned departure from work.

If you have been following up the examples used throughout this book by composing your own list of long-term needs, you are well on the way to planning your retirement. With this information in hand, you are now ready to use it in order to set up the framework by which you can investigate and analyze retirement opportunities. And you thought we would never get to this point!

Your past *and* your present are critical to planning your future.

Your Current State of Affairs

If you are like many people, your list of needs includes some that are being well met in your present life as well as those needs that are being partially or not-at-all met. In addition, since retirement will thrust some lifestyle changes upon you, it is likely that this balance of met and unmet needs will change as your personal circumstances change. This is the point where your long-term needs intersect with your present or projected life circumstances and necessitate decision-making—in this case, retirement decision-making.

The first step in investigating where you want to go is to decide where you are, rather like those maps in large shopping centers with an arrow that says, "You are here." In short, you must compare the long-term needs that you have with the situations in your present work and nonwork life that allow for the satisfaction of these needs. As well as providing you with a "baseline" that will help you to understand the impact of possible future decisions, this can also aid you in understanding the motivation you might have to undertake such changes—the driving power of your unmet needs.

The process used to evaluate the need-satisfying power of your current life circumstances is the opposite of the process you have used thus far. In this case, you start with the needs you have identified and look for activities—things you are currently doing in your work and nonwork life—that satisfy these needs for you. In doing so, you will be able to identify those of your needs that do not have enough activities associated with them for the need to be satisfied. As a side effect you might also discover a variety of activities you are engaged in that do not appear to satisfy any of your needs—time wasters.

Here, by way of example, are a sample of the results from Harry, an owner of a small local chain of automobile specialty shops who was considering retirement at age fifty-five.

Need	Work Activities	Nonwork Activities
Intellect	"I think the only thing that requires brains in what I am doing now is figuring out how to keep everybody working hard. I am not considering expanding and everything else just sort of runs itself."	"I have always been a reader, primarily of war history, and I enjoy talking about the tactics of war with somebody who knows what they are talking about. I am also a kind of amateur inventor and can fix just about anything that breaks. I am also a puzzle junkie and diddle away at all kinds of puzzles when I am bored."
Competition	"This business is cut-throat, particularly now, and even us old timers can't take anything for granted. I enjoy deal-making with suppliers and spending every nickel twice. Everything I do now pits me against somebody or something."	"I don't have much outside of work. I used to golf but gave that up because of my legs. Maybe a bit from some church fund-raising I am doing just now."
Recognition	"I guess I get plenty from work. I have twice won the local award for 'Business of the Year' and I have just been asked to run for the local govern-	"I am in a service club but I am no different from anybody else. I don't know, I guess in the community I am known as 'Harry—the car man.'

Need	Work Activities	Nonwork Activities
	ment, primarily because of my business contacts. I guess my employees also know I am the boss!"	I have done my own ads on TV and most people here know who I am."
Materialism	"I do okay from the business. It has ups and downs but mostly I have been lucky—so far."	"I have quiet money invested in several other business situations that I will hold onto even if I retire. I won't be hurting and I don't suppose the town will have to pay to bury me!"
Affiliation	"I am with people all the time, employees, customers, suppliers, you-name-it. There is always a bustle of people when I am around."	"I try to get away from people when I am not working. I spend some time with my son's kids when I can and I go to church. That's about it."
Adventure	"At work, there is always something happening. I try to buy out other places in the area that have gone bankrupt and I still get a kick out of running my three stores."	"I do some fishing and a bit of hunting and I enjoy that but I don't know if you would call that Adventure."

Even with the small sample of Harry's present activities, it is easy to see that if he retired point-blank, without any advance preparation so far as his needs are concerned, he would experience considerable difficulty. Much of his needs satisfaction is tied up with his business, and his business has also kept him so involved that he has not developed many nonwork activities that are likely to provide him with sufficient opportunities to meet his needs.

Although Harry's Intellect needs do not seem to be well met through work, and his Materialism needs are satisfied through work and nonwork, the same thing is not true for his other needs. Where, for example, should Harry look to satisfy his strong needs for Competition, Recognition, Affiliation, and Adventure if he retires? It is these areas where he must direct his search for nonwork opportunities if he is serious about his intent to retire—and wants to remain sane while doing so.

Here is another sample of the same exercise for Darlene, a department manager in the local branch of a national department store. She will retire in six months at the mandated age of sixty-five.

Need	Work Activities	Nonwork Activities
Affiliation	"I have never been much of a 'joiner' at work. I think what I still enjoy the most is contact with the customers, talking with them and trying to help them. I do enjoy training new staff and working closely with them when they are starting out."	"My husband and I took up lawn bowling several years ago and I really enjoy the people. I also spend as much time as I can with my two daughters and their children. We have a cottage at the lake and in the summertime there always seems to be people around."
Competition	"Funny thing is, I never used to think that I was competitive at work but I guess I am. I always like to compare my figures with those of the other department managers and I am always setting daily sales goals in my own mind."	"I suppose that lawn bowling is competitive in a way and I am very fussy about my flower gardens to make them the best in the neighborhood. I don't think there are many avenues to be competitive at home."

Need	Work Activities	Nonwork Activities
Intellect	"My work is pretty routine now. The store is not growing or changing very much. When there are decisions that require much thought, I never get to make them anyway."	"I think I must be missing out on this area at home pretty much also. Most things I do, I just do and I don't have to think about them very much now—I don't have to plan or puzzle through them."
Influence	"I really like managing a department. I guess I like telling people what to do. I can pretty much set things up the way I want although I do have to adhere to company policies. Maybe that is why I like training the new staff—I can get to see the effects of my ideas."	"Other than managing a husband, I don't know how much influence I have away from work. I know I don't have much any more with my children. I am not active in clubs or associations to any degree and I have even resisted getting involved in the lawn bowling club—except for the bowling."
Aesthetics	"Before I was department manager, I was in charge of store displays and I really enjoyed that. I still do some of that now within my own department and I enjoy it very much."	"I sometimes do some 'artsy' photography work although I probably did more earlier in my life. I guess my flower garden is my major outlet at least in the summertime."

Need	Work Activities	Nonwork Activities
Adventure	"There is not much of that in my work. Twice a year, I get to travel to head office when we introduce the new spring and fall fashions and I like to do that."	"My husband and I have traveled but that has always been as tourists. There is very little adventure in my day-to-day life."

In comparing Darlene's results to those of Harry, some interesting differences emerge. Like Harry, Darlene relies on her work for the primary satisfaction of some of her needs, particularly Influence and Aesthetics. Unlike Harry, she has some needs, particularly Adventure and Intellect, that do not appear to be well satisfied through her current work *or* nonwork activities. Since Darlene has no choice in her retirement decision, her challenge will be to seek retirement opportunities that fill in the void that work will leave for her but also to seek those opportunities that can supplement deficits in her present life circumstances that are not being met by either work or nonwork activities.

RETIREMENT EXERCISE 9

Using your list of needs you have already identified itemize the *activities you currently pursue* in your work and nonwork life that provide for the meeting of your needs. Remember you are not focusing on what you *could do* to meet these needs but what you *actually do*.

The first step in investigating where you want to go was to examine the activities you currently use in your life to meet your needs. Step Two is to examine the impact of removing the middle column, "Work Activities," from your list of need-satisfying situations in your current life. That is the position you would be in should you be unavoidably retired tomorrow and left with only

"Nonwork Activities" as means to meet your needs. For instance, in the example of Harry, most of his important needs are being met through work and it would be expected that considerable adjustment would be necessary in making an unplanned transition to retirement. Although different needs would be impacted, the same thing is true in the example of Darlene.

For most people, removing work from the picture as a means to meet needs is very significant and it can sometimes be a little frightening to realize how much you have depended on work situations to meet your needs. On the other hand, you may find that removal of work opportunities has a neglegible impact on the satisfaction of your needs, a fact that usually indicates dissatisfaction with your present work situation. That's probably good news for retirement planning but bad news for your present work situation.

It is the need-satisfying power of work that many people underestimate in their retirement planning. Such underestimation can result in the "postretirement blues" so common once the initial glow has worn off the retirement rose. The individuals so afflicted know that something is missing in their lives but either tell themselves that they should not feel this way or cannot articulate their feelings. They are unhappy because they are longing for lost opportunity.

An additional complicating factor for many people is that, in addition to the loss of work resulting in the loss of opportunities to meet their needs, retirement usually results in some modification of their nonwork activities as well. A relocation to a new community may be necessary, economic circumstances may be diminished, or work-related affiliations may be modified. Taken alone, any of these modifications would be stressful because it results in diminished opportunities to meet their needs. When added to the stress resulting from the loss of work opportunities, the effect is magnified.

An unplanned retirement that results in many of your needs-satisfying opportunities disappearing with nothing to take their place can have the same effects as the sudden and unexpected death of a spouse—loss and bewilderment—but it need not happen to you.

Certainly, the work-related activities you have identified as important in meeting your needs will no longer be available to you once you retire. But you can be satisfied in your retirement by finding new opportunities in other aspects of your life to replace those that will be lost. To do otherwise, to pretend that you do not have needs that are partially met through work, is folly. As the man selling preventative maintenance for automobiles preaches on the television, "you can pay me now or you can pay me later."

Retirement will not change your needs. It will change only the opportunities you have available to meet your needs.

Chapter 7

Responding to Opportunities

"For age is opportunity no less
Than youth itself."
—Henry Wadsworth Longfellow, "Morituri Salutamus"

Responding to opportunities is a lot like responding lucidly to other people's witty remarks. Before you realize what has happened, the chance to act appropriately has disappeared. In hindsight, I am twenty-twenty and I am still waiting for the smart aleck who commented disparagingly on my spreading waistline to make the same comment again. Boy, will I zap her this time!

In responding to life's opportunities, most of us have that same twenty-twenty hindsight. But, like all "roads not taken," it is too easy to glamorize a choice not made, too easy to pine away with thoughts of what could have been. I am sure that I could do better at relating to my parents, getting ahead at my job, raising my children, or managing my finances—next time. I am not certain what I would do differently but I sometimes think with regret of that job offer on the western seaboard I turned down, that pretty young undergraduate with dishonorable intentions I failed in her sophomore year, or, worse yet, turning down a chance to buy IBM at its issue price! If only, if only, if only . . .

On the other hand, there are some "golden opportunities" I did act upon that I now wish had gone the way of my IBM stock option. Does anybody out there want to buy some gold at $900 an ounce? If so, I will throw in an old accepted job offer from the Cutthroat School System as an added bonus. Sometimes it is easy now to understand my father when he suggested I should "sit that one out."

My problem is one of sitting when I should have run and running when I should have sat!

But, it is thinking like this that really gets you into trouble: responding to past mistakes with present inactivity, the old "I can't make a mistake if I don't do nothin' " philosophy. Unfortunately the only way to *guarantee* that you will "sit when you should have sat" is to sit, and sit, and sit. And that itself may prove to be a mistake.

A Tale of Two Lifestyles

Russell

To say that Russell, fifty-eight going on seventy, was unenthused with his job, with his whole lot in life, is like saying northern Canada has chilly winters. A senior social worker with a large government department, Russell was part of a vanishing breed of worker who started his career with one employer and was still there some thirty-plus years later. Not that he wanted to be there, not that he had to be there, but he was there. Russell's specialty was welfare fraud and he was an acknowledged technical expert in his field, having pioneered the use of sophisticated statistical analysis for early detection of suspicious cases.

At three different points in his long career with the government department, Russell had been offered attractive positions with other employers, one with a government agency in a larger jurisdiction and two others with private consulting agencies providing fraud detection services on a contractual basis. Each time, although he wanted to make the move, he hesitated, and hesitated and hesitated. "Maybe," he said, "I won't like it." Eventually, all three offers "disappeared."

Now, as a result of cutbacks, Russell was part of the fifty-five-plus category of workers eligible for full early retirement from his government department. He disliked his work, seemed unhappy with his life in general. But still he hesitated. "Maybe," he reiterated in the interview, "I won't like it."

Jean

Jean, sixty, seemed to have the energy and vitality of a woman half her age. At present the executive producer for a large midwestern television station, she had held many positions in her more than thirty-five years of work, including a goodly amount of time off from paid work to raise two sons. A teacher by training, she had entered the television business more by accident than by design as a result of her amateur dramatic productions at a time when television was gaining a toe-hold in the entertainment industry. And Jean had flourished, making several career moves to larger and larger stations, moving through both creative and management positions with skill and enthusiasm.

Jean's husband of some forty years was her senior by five years and was about to be retired from his position with a national firm of engineering consultants. Although they lived in the Midwest, they had often talked of returning to the eastern seaboard on retirement, although they had never identified precisely when that would be.

Jean was initially uncertain about whether or not she could leave a job she enjoyed for the uncertainties of a retirement she did not yet feel ready for. Her husband put no pressure on her to have their move coincide with his retirement but it did seem like a natural breaking-off point.

"Maybe this would be a good thing to do now," she commented. "I've always thought you should quit when you were ahead—before they hold the door open for you!" As Jean considered the idea further she was able to identify a number of things she could do if she did make the move now. "I think I would get involved with drama again in some way, perhaps with kids this time. That is something I miss in television and it would give me the chance to run something I would like to run."

By the time Jean and her husband had made their move to the East, some eight months later, she had contacted three of the professional and semiprofessional drama groups in their chosen location and had discovered a real opportunity with one semi-professional group that was initiating a school-based drama education program. "They were just waiting for someone like me," she said, beaming. "I can hardly wait to try it."

Russell and Jean portray two very different ways of looking at life's opportunities. In Russell's case, life is not comprised of opportunities. Life is a series of events with the individual as a passive and sometimes unwilling participant. Russell does not *choose* for things to happen to him. Things happen by default largely as a result of his dithering. Jean is proactive. She acts on the assumption that it is her choices that will affect her destiny. Jean views the future positively because she is willing to actively make decisions and compromises by pursuing opportunities that she thinks will make her happy.

Success in retirement is not something to be strived for directly. It is the natural by-product of meeting your needs and maximizing the opportunities that come your way.

The only absolutely certain way to assess whether or not you should take advantage of a situation that confronts you is by grabbing the situation, running with it, and assessing the results months or years down the line. Obviously, it is neither possible nor wise to behave in such an undifferentiated fashion for every possible opportunity. But it is also unwise to do nothing in response to all of life's opportunities. The sit-this-one-out choice that results from the vain hope of avoiding the negative effects of a decision precludes receiving any possible benefits from whatever results. You can't win the lottery if you don't buy the ticket.

What Does an Opportunity Look Like?

There are opportunities and then there are opportunities, and it is often difficult to tell one from another. As well, some opportunities are foisted upon us by life's circumstances and it is not so much a question of actively pursuing them as it is of deciding whether or not you will allow yourself to be caught. The trick is to recognize an opportunity when it presents itself as well as being able to recognize a favorable set of circumstances that you can exploit in creating an opportunity where one is not immediately evident.

A dictionary definition of an opportunity relates it to a favorable juncture of circumstances, something you feel would result in positive outcomes for you. *Defined in terms of your retirement planning, an opportunity is an alternative or possibility that could lead to the meeting of some of your needs.* The difficulty with a strict definition of an opportunity is that it covers just about every life circumstance you could imagine, and although it is theoretically possible for every life circumstance to be an opportunity, that is usually not the case.

For an alternative or possibility to be an opportunity for you, it must allow for the meeting of one or more of your needs *but* it must not preclude you from meeting other important needs that cannot be accommodated in other ways. Put simply, there must be a *net positive benefit* to you in terms of needs satisfaction for an apparent opportunity to be real. It is ignorance of this refined definition of an opportunity that explains the disillusionment we have all experienced in pursuing opportunities that end up more ethereal than real. Such is often the case with individuals who, apparently aimlessly, pursue a series of failed intimate relationships, jobs, or living accommodations. They pursue rainbows without believing in rainstorms.

Most people do not recognize their opportunities because they do not understand their needs.

We see the clearest example of the effects of ignoring this "net positive benefit" rule in the workplace where many individuals view a possible job advancement to positions of greater authority solely in terms of the greater opportunity to meet needs such as Influence, Recognition, or Materialism without assessing the impact on needs such as Affiliation, Security, or Intellect. Situations such as this account for the unhappiness of many middle executives who have progressed to their current positions by a combination of their own talent and someone else's idea of what should make them happy.

This mistake is also evident in the retirement plans of some people. It shows itself in a decision to retire and make wholesale changes in lifestyle without thinking through the implications of such changes. It is also evident in retirements where nothing is planned to accommodate for the diminished or modified opportunities that result from amputating an important aspect of one's life—paid work.

David was an account executive for a national firm of billboard advertisers. Although he was only average in performance, he enjoyed his job a great deal and gained considerable pleasure from his customer contacts as well as the regional travel necessitated by his work.

Approaching sixty-five, David was scheduled to retire at the end of the year. He attended a retirement planning seminar sponsored by his firm although he indicated that, "aside from the financial information, I can't see what other dope I need."

During the detailed personal needs assessment that formed a major part of the retirement seminar, it became evident that David's strong Affiliation, Competition and Recognition needs were being met mainly through his work activities. To complicate matters, there appeared to be few opportunities in his current nonwork life circumstances that would allow for these needs to be met in other ways.

David was initially disbelieving of the importance of his needs and indicated that he "didn't see any problems in retiring." He left the seminar with only sketchy half-hearted plans for the psychological side of his retirement although he did admit that he found the financial information useful.

I next met David on a personal consultation basis about a year later, some six months after he had retired. Things were not going well for him. He reported that he often found himself "at wit's end" in terms of doing anything that was meaningful and he frequently ended up in bars commiserating with his cronies, thus reviving a drinking problem he had licked some twenty years earlier. "I'm bored, bored silly," he admitted.

It is unlikely that you can capitalize on all of life's opportunities that come your way. Nor can you expect to arrange all of life's circumstances so that you can always create opportunities when you need them. Nobody bats a thousand in meeting their needs but successful people do not strike out every time either. Luckily, the human character is robust enough to stand a good deal of error or sloppiness in meeting personal needs. Still, it is best not to push your luck too far!

Your needs provide you with the framework to explore opportunities and examine options.

Guidelines for Recognizing Your Opportunities

It is *recognizing* opportunities or circumstances that you can turn into opportunities that many people find difficult. This is because such recognition must take place in what a computer person would call "real time"—when you can still do something about it. Let us look at a few guidelines that can aid you in your quest for opportunities.

1. If you cannot identify your needs you will not be able to identify your opportunities. I have said it before and I will say it again: Opportunities do not exist in a vacuum. Unless you can relate

potential opportunities to personal needs you will always fall victim to someone else defining your opportunities for you. Your needs are important because it is impossible to realistically evaluate the wealth of opportunities that confront the average person without having some framework within which such evaluations can be made. If you are not aware of your needs, the success of your retirement will be a matter of luck—and luck is not always of the positive kind.

2. There are two dimensions to an opportunity: the projected benefit and the projected cost. These two dimensions are inseparable and although you may sometimes talk yourself into believing you can get the benefit without the cost, it just ain't so. In terms of retirement planning the costs are usually negative side-effects that may prevent you from meeting other important needs you have. For example, an opportunity to fulfill an Adventure need usually has some negative effects in terms of meeting a Security need. The effects may not be disastrous—something as simple as arranging for home security during your safari to Africa—but such effects must be reckoned with and accommodated.

3. There is a general truism that says your needs will not be met through any activity unless you have the skills to perform with adequate competence at that activity. This means that an opportunity is only an opportunity for you if you have at least the minimum skills required to take advantage of it. Although perfection is not a requisite, a need is not met by doing something poorly. For example, the evaluation of an opportunity to start a part-time business after retiring must be predicated on a skill level sufficient to undertake that business satisfactorily. If the need that drives you to such activity is strong in spite of your diminished competence, and if no other means are available to meet the need, you should improve your skills.

4. The satisfaction level of other people undertaking an opportunity can provide little guidance to you in your selection of that opportunity. Since it is impossible to determine what needs

other individuals are meeting in pursuing an opportunity you are considering, their satisfaction or dissatisfaction with that opportunity will provide you with little guidance in making your own choice. I have a spare trumpet, flute, and trombone because all three "looked like fun" when somebody else was using them.

5. Opportunities always seem to arise when they are least expected and decisions must usually be made quickly or the chance is lost. A corollary of this is that it is difficult or impossible to determine your needs and assess a potential opportunity at the same time. In such cases, needs are usually identified in terms of the opportunity rather than the other way around. Don't wait until your professional association asks you to head a task force "now that you're retired" before you try to decide what you need out of life. Unless you know what you need, forget about exploring or evaluating options to get it.

6. Many viable opportunities involve modifications or modest changes in what you are already doing. Although it is grandiose wholesale changes that are often the most seducing, it is the smaller changes that often yield the most net benefit. Maybe you don't need to move to the French Riviera, divorce your spouse, or go to college in order to be happy when you retire. Maybe you need to do something as simple as ensuring that you will have ongoing task-oriented contact with people now that work has removed that formal contact with people from your life.

7. Opportunities often exist in close association with problems and are usually related to the solution of those problems. This truism is particularly appropriate in business situations but it is also very relevant to the consideration of retirement options. Maybe a difficulty in paying additional municipal taxes can lead to an opportunity in organizing a lobby group, thus satisfying needs such as Influence or Recognition—and lowering your taxes in the bargain! Maybe poor service in a restaurant can lead to a part-time business opportunity providing consulting serv-

ices to restaurants. But while every cloud may have a silver lining, it is a lining that must be searched for!

8. Most opportunities involve two kinds of risk. The first risk is that you will not be successful in undertaking whatever is necessary to take advantage of the opportunity. The second risk is that you will be successful but that the net benefits will be less than expected. If you cannot stand risks, forget about opportunities but remember that most risks are not either-or. You are neither successful or unsuccessful, will neither be happy or unhappy. Do not minimize the risks of your retirement decision-making but don't let your worry about such risks cripple you from taking any action.

9. Opportunities impact on those with whom you have intimate relationships. What might be a very viable opportunity for you as an individual might pale when you consider the impact on your marriage or family relationships. The needs of intimate individuals are usually symbiotic and it is perilous for your relationships to consider an opportunity for yourself without considering the impact on those around you. Nothing is as wearying as an unhappy house-mate.

10. Most opportunities that are not gut-wrenching in their possible negative side effects are usually better taken rather than not taken if you find yourself unable to make an unambiguous choice. This is the advice of others far older and wiser than I who report more long-term anguish about opportunities not taken than they do about opportunities that were taken but which did not work out. It really is better to have loved and lost than never to have loved at all!

What Is Jane's Opportunity?

Jane, a fifty-eight-year-old professor of business at a large university on the East Coast, was a recent participant at a retirement planning seminar. She was eligible for retirement within two years and was experiencing a good deal of difficulty in evaluating the options available to her.

During the course of her teaching career, Jane had pursued an active consulting practice, primarily with eastern-based government organizations and large corporations. She had recently married for a third time to a man two years her junior.

"I would like to move back to California but I don't know if that would work out. I've thought of continuing my consulting work after I leave the university but all of my contacts are here so maybe California wouldn't be a good idea. My husband says he does not care what we do. He has even agreed to retire from his job a few years early but I don't want him to have to do that."

To make matters more complicated, one of Jane's friends, a colleague at a college in California, had recently written her encouraging Jane to return to California and holding forth the opportunity of some part-time work at a local college. Her friend had also indicated that part-time consulting activities should be "no problem" in California as she was heavily involved in that area herself.

Jane is drawn by the possibility of a move to California, can almost "smell the surf at Malibu" in her dreams. Economically, such a move is certainly possible and her husband is apparently agreeable. A friend has started lobbying her for a positive decision and promises further financial and professional rewards. So why not move?

Most times, our decisions are like those of Jane. We are drawn and repelled by the same possibility and yet we know we must make a decision that is unidimensional—a decision that either accepts or rejects a potential opportunity. Even when we are able to look realistically at the positive and negative effects of the proposed decision, nagging doubts always linger. These are the doubts that accompany change. We have a certain knowledge that any decision, no matter how good it looks, involves some disruption in a routine that, while it may not be perfect, is predictable.

Nothing you can do will totally *remove* doubt from your retirement planning. At best you can hope to *control* it. You exert that control by assessing very carefully the true impact of decisions you might make in taking advantage of opportunities. But you must do more than this. You must also be prepared to pursue new opportunities—opportunities that are not confronting you at present—to fill the voids that are a natural by-product of prior decisions you have made. For while it is true that every opportunity demands a decision, making that decision will require you to pursue other opportunities and make other decisions.

Chapter 8

Opportunities
+ Pursuit
= Success

"Nothing succeeds like success."
—Alexandre Dumas, *Ange Pitou*

There is nothing "natural" about retirement. You are not born knowing how to do it, and knowing how will not come to you with the gold watch. That being said, there are still many people who are doing an admirable job of it, who report retirement as "the best years of their lives." Almost without exception, such people see retirement as the "best years" because they are doing something to make it so. The most striking characteristic of those who make the successful transition from work to retirement is that they are what I call "opportunity pursuers." Sometimes consciously, or with calculation—more often unconsciously, or incognizant—they *pursue opportunities* that meet their needs. For them, opportunities + pursuit = success.

Conversely, there are individuals, perhaps you know some of them or are one yourself, for whom retirement is spelled m-i-s-e-r-y. Sometimes that misery is a result of actively pursuing opportunities that are either inappropriate or unattainable. More often, it is a result of *not* pursuing those opportunities that might be appropriate or could be attainable. According to the equation, remember, success requires two factors—pursuit and opportunity—and one without the other simply cannot lead to positive results.

It is probably easier to assess the opportunity value of a situation that is confronting you than it is to seek out or create an opportunity where one does not exist. In the first case, the situation is staring you squarely in the face and your job is to weigh the implications of either pursuing or not pursuing. In the second case, you start from a different position, your needs, and cast about looking for new situations that will allow your needs to be met. In the first case, you are evaluating a specific. In the second case, you are looking for a specific to evaluate.

Pursuing opportunities is like courtship. Without a program, it is hard to tell the pursued from the pursuer.

Steven

Steven, aged fifty-five, was employed in an academic administrative position with a mid-sized public university. Previous to this position, which he had held for fifteen years, Steven had been an elementary school teacher, and later a high school teacher. He held pension entitlements with the school system and the university.

Two events had unfolded that presented Steven with a unique opportunity for full early retirement. The first situation was an agreement with the teachers' association that all teachers could retire on full pension after thirty years of service. The second was an agreement between the university and the school system that allowed for a reciprocal exchange of pension rights for newly recruited employees with a certain minimum length of service with the other employer.

Although his university did not allow for full pension until sixty-five, with reduced benefits available at sixty, Steven was able to recognize a loophole in the two agreements—a loophole that would be to his decided benefit should he wish to retire early. It was possible, he reasoned, to resign his position with the university, secure a teaching position for the minimum six-month peroid, and thereby transfer his pension benefits to the lucrative teachers' plan, with full recognition for his years of university service. If he did so, he could then retire early on the teachers' plan with thirty years of service.

This seemed like a unique opportunity and yet Steven hesitated. "You know, when it all comes down to this, I am not sure I want to retire, even though I have always talked about it."

Steven had just completed a retirement planning seminar and was surprised to identify that a number of his needs, particularly Affiliation, Competition, and Influence, were being met almost exclusively through his work.

"Here I have an excellent practical opportunity, one that will probably disappear in a few years, and yet I wonder if it is a real opportunity for me?"

Steven's story has a happy ending. He decided the "practical opportunity" was too good a deal to pass up. (In fact, the loophole was modified soon after he used it). However, in the six final months that Steven spent working within the school system, he worked almost as hard in seeking out alternative ways to deal with his needs that would no longer be possible to meet through work. By the time he actually retired, Steven had taken advantage of an opportunity for a small amount of ongoing part-time teaching, had moved into a leadership position within his service club, and had decided to pursue part-time training for voluntary pastoral duties within his church. "Some retirement," he joked, "but I think it will work for me."

Steven's story demonstrates a key point about opportunities. Very often the decision to take advantage of an opportunity that is confronting you must be followed up by your pursuit of other opportunities to fill in the gaps left by the first opportunity. Seldom does a perfect opportunity ever exist in a vacuum and the benefits of pursuing an opportunity that confronts you must be balanced by actively seeking out opportunities that are not immediately evident. To do otherwise is to trade one kind of dissatisfaction for another.

This key point comes about because the pursuit of a particular opportunity often means that you must *change elements of your present life that currently meet some of your needs* in order to take advantage of the new opportunity. This means that it is not just the opportunity that will introduce change into your life; it is *what you must modify in your current life* to take advantage of that opportunity, what additional new opportunities you will be required to seek out in order to achieve a balance. The problem is that, when confronted by an opportunity, most people see what they could be getting without giving much thought to what they might have to give up.

The other side of the coin is that you must not let the possibility of undesirable side effects in opting for an opportunity freeze you into nonaction. In most cases, it is possible to work around minor side-effects, to identify ways of dealing with the unpleasant implications of pursuing your dreams.

Dana

Dana was employed in a middle management position with the postal service. Although as a young man he had worked in several locations across the country, he eventually settled in a midwestern agricultural community where he worked for more than thirty years. Perhaps in deference to his own rural upbringing, Dana had chosen to live on a small acreage some fifteen miles from his work. Now at sixty, Dana was eligible for full retirement and had spent a good deal of time examining his options.

"I don't think I am the kind of person who can just stop—like that," he volunteered during an employer-sponsored retirement seminar. In fact, a more detailed needs assessment conducted as part of the workshop indicated that he was quite correct in that assertion. He had strong Competition, Security, Recognition, Influence, and Affiliation needs, all of which were met to some extent through his work.

After further discussion, it became evident that Security needs would not be a concern should Dana retire, provided that retirement did not necessitate other major changes such as a relocation. In addition, Affiliation needs were only modestly met through work and it was Dana's opinion that these needs could likely be met through more extensive involvement with the local and regional amateur radio fraternity, a hobby he had pursued since his high school days.

Dana's focus then turned to Competition, Recognition, and Influence needs, all of which were important and, thus far, met largely through his work. "I need to have projects, something I can get my teeth into, before I am happy," Dana volunteered to the retirement seminar. He left the seminar knowing what he wanted but with only modest progress in enunciating how he would get it.

I next heard of Dana a year later when he responded in an extensive written fashion to a follow-up survey of retirement seminar participants. "I spent a lot of time investigating possibilities and discarding most of them," he wrote. "I began to feel that it might be hopeless, that I might just have to put up with not having what I knew I wanted—even if I didn't know how to get it."

Dana went on to report that his opportunity had come from a most unlikely source. A younger neighbor who owned a larger acreage adjacent to Dana had decided to relocate to another part of the country and offered his thriving part-time "cottage industry" bee-keeping business to Dana at a fire-sale price. Although he had only minimal experience with bees, the idea immediately attracted Dana and he decided to puchase the business.

"I am very busy now and probably happier than when I was working for the post office," Dana continued in his letter. "I think some of my neighbors think I am nuts for starting this so late in life but I enjoy it. And business is good—better than when my neighbor did it. I've even had to hire two high-school students part-time when things get busy."

Dana's story and that of every other successful retiree share one point in common. No needs can be met by inactivity. Meeting of needs is a by-product of *doing something*. It is not important that what you do be large scale, world class, or expensive, but only that you take the initiative. Perhaps Shakespeare's Lear said it most succinctly: "Nothing will come of nothing."

If "nothing comes of nothing," the problem insofar as opportunities are concerned is choosing something to replace those opportunities that will be lost through your loss of work. As well, since few of us are at a perfectly balanced point with respect to our needs before we retire, it may also mean searching for opportunities that will meet needs that are not currently being met with or without our work.

Steps in Evaluating Opportunities

Here are a few specific steps for seeking and evaluating opportunities. Do not follow them just yet. Wait until you read the two examples that ensue.

1. Look at your list of long-term needs and identify those needs that are being met mainly through your work. Include in this list needs that, although they may not be met directly through work, are met by virtue of your position as a worker. For example, you may find that needs such as Recognition and Influence, which are being largely met through your community involvement, are able to be met in this way only because of your position as an employee of your company.

2. Supplement this list with those of your long-term needs that are not being well met at present through work *or* nonwork pursuits.

3. Pretending that you are now no longer working (and are therefore unable to meet any of your needs through work), assess the degree of unmet needs satisfaction you might expect for each of the needs identified in Steps 1 and 2. You may decide, for example, that an important need might be only minimally affected by leaving work or that, conversely, a middle-strength need might be affected a great deal. What you will end up with is not a list of your needs but rather a

list of your unmet needs, and the strength of each one, in the event of your leaving work.

4. If you are actively considering concrete opportunities at the present time, subject each potential opportunity to the scrutiny of how well that opportunity would assist you to meet your unmet needs in the event of your leaving work. In addition, identify how taking advantage of each opportunity might adversely affect needs that are already being fully satisfied.

5. If you have a number of potential opportunities "in the back of your mind," subject each one to the same scrutiny as you did for your concrete opportunities.

6. Evaluate the practical possibility of undertaking the opportunities you identified in Steps 4 and 5. Discard possibilities that, although they might meet your needs, are clearly impossible because of practical considerations.

7. Based on the premise that you will actually undertake the opportunities not discarded in Step 6, revise your list of unmet needs identified in Step 3. Be sure to reconsider those of your met needs that might be adversely affected by taking advantage of potential opportunities.

8. Investigate other opportunities to meet your revised list of unmet needs identified in Step 7 (more about how to do this later).

9. Repeat Steps 6 and 7 for those opportunities identified in Step 8.

10. Repeat Steps 8 and 9 as often as required.

Two Examples

To help you in working through these ten steps, here are two examples. The first is Ted, a fifty-seven-year-old owner of a small electrical contracting company. Ted is considering retirement, partly on the advise of his doctor, because of persistent back problems aggravated by the strenuous nature of his work. These problems are not severe enough to affect his general mobility and nonwork lifestyle.

The second example is Marion, a fifty-six-year-old senior librarian, currently employed as head librarian with a large municipal library. Marion, a recent widow, is considering retirement on a somewhat accelerated schedule since the death of her husband has resulted in sizeable insurance and spousal-retirement benefits accruing to her.

1. Make a list of your long-term needs that are being mainly met through your work.

   Ted

   Influence
   Competition
   Materialism
   Freedom
   Recognition

   Marion

   Recognition
   Influence
   Affiliation
   Intellect
   Security

2. Supplement this list with those of your long-term needs that are not being well met at present through work *or* nonwork pursuits.

   Ted

   Aesthetics
   Altruism
   Affiliation

   Marion

   Altruism
   Religion
   Adventure

3. Pretending that you are now no longer working (and are therefore unable to meet any of your needs through work), assess the degree of unmet needs satisfaction you might expect for each of the needs identified in Steps 1 and 2.

Ted

Influence	Medium
Competition	High
Materialism	Low
Freedom	Low
Recognition	High
Aesthetics	Medium
Altruism	Medium
Affiliation	Medium

Marion

Recognition	Medium
Influence	High
Affiliation	High
Intellect	High
Security	Low
Altruism	Medium
Religion	Medium
Adventure	High

4. If you are actively considering concrete opportunities at the present time, subject each potential opportunity to the scrutiny of how well that opportunity would assist you to meet your unmet needs in the event of your leaving work. In addition, identify how taking advantage of each opportunity might adversely affect needs that are already being fully satisfied.

Ted

Concrete Opportunity	Effects

Considering selling the business to youngest son (at a fair price) and moving to the West Coast. Eldest son and daughter live there with their families.

Provide additional time for the meeting of Aesthetics needs through long-abandoned hobby of painting.

Would meet Freedom needs through lack of structure and work expectations of others.

Might adversely affect Security and Affiliation needs because of the stress of relocation. On the other hand, Security needs would be enhanced through closer contact with children and grandchildren.

Would impact only marginally on other met and unmet needs.

Marion

Concrete Opportunity	Effects

Undertaking a two-year assignment with a United Nations agency to set up library services in a developing university in a third-world country.

Strong positive effects on Adventure, Intellect, Altruism, Influence, and Recognition needs.

Possible negative effects on Affiliation and Security needs resulting from relocation in a foreign country.

5. If you have a number of potential opportunities "in the back of your mind," subject each one to the same scrutiny as you did for your concrete opportunities.

Ted

Potential Opportunities	Effects

A. Providing free consulting service to senior citizens who might be taken advantage of by unscrupulous electrical contractors.

Would probably aid in meeting Influence, Recognition, and Altruism needs and provide for some minimal satisfaction of Competition needs.

No negative effects are foreseen.

B. Learning to golf.

Would probably help in meeting Competition needs and might assist in meeting Affiliation needs expected to be disrupted if relocation is undertaken.

C. Write a how-to book for consumers on how to avoid getting "ripped off" in dealing with electrical contractors.

Would probably help to meet Recognition and Influence needs and, to a lesser extent, Altruism needs.

Marion

Potential Opportunities	Effects

A. Considering moving to another city to live with twin sister, who lost her husband three years earlier.

Would aid in the meeting of Affiliation and Security needs because Marion and her sister were very close. Some potential for negative effects for these same needs because of relocation.

Some short-term positive effects in terms of Adventure need because of excitement in moving to a new city.

Potential Opportunities	Effects
B. Recently announced changes within her church had prompted Marion to consider volunteer part-time lay ministerial work in her home town.	Would aid in the meeting of Religion and Altruism needs as well as providing some opportunity to meet Recognition and Influence needs.
	Would probably exaggerate lack of opportunity to meet Adventure needs.
C. A recently announced policy at the municipal level had made it possible for managers to "phase into retirement" by reducing their employment (and salary) by one-half in the five years preceding retirement. Marion was eligible for this alternative.	Aside from giving Marion more free time to pursue other opportunities, she was unable to identify any specific needs this opportunity would meet. As well, she identified a possible negative outcome in terms of her Affiliation needs because of the reduced contact with her co-workers.

6. Evaluate the practical possibility of undertaking the concrete and potential opportunities you have identified in Steps 4 and 5. Discard possibilities that, although they might meet your needs, are clearly impossible because of practical considerations.

Ted

With the possible exception of the book-writing opportunity, the others are judged to be practically possible. Ted had never written anything major before and had only high school education. He was somewhat uncertain as to how to begin or if he could do it even though he had the ideas.

Marion

In Marion's case, she was left with a choice of pursuing her present opportunity (Step 4) or one or more of her possibilities since the two kinds of opportunity were mutually exclusive. She decided to focus her evaluation on the possibility of foreign service, particularly since it was a once-in-a-lifetime opportunity and since there were some practical constraints posed by the other possible alternatives.

7. Based on the premise that you will actually undertake the opportunities not discarded in Step 6, revise your list of unmet needs you identified in Step 3. Be sure to reconsider those of your met needs that might be adversely affected by taking advantage of potential opportunities.

Ted

Influence	Low
Competition	Medium-High
Materialism	Low
Freedom	Low
Recognition	Medium
Aesthetics	Low
Altruism	Low
Affiliation	Medium

Marion

Recognition	Low
Influence	Low
Affiliation	Medium-High
Intellect	Low
Security	Medium
Altruism	Low
Religion	Medium
Adventure	Low

8. Investigate other opportunities to meet your revised list of unmet needs identified in Step 7.

Ted

At this point, Ted did not feel capable of completing Steps 8 to 10 because he could not think of other potential opportunities.

Marion

Although she knew what additional needs she was seeking to meet, Marion did not yet have any firm ideas for opportunities she might pursue to meet them. She focused on opportunities she might pursue in the third-world country where her original opportunity would lead her but lacked the detailed knowledge of the country and culture necessary to make informed judgments.

It is evident that Ted will still need to address his Competition and Affiliation needs even if he takes full advantage of the opportunities he has listed—even if these opportunities work out the way he thinks they will. Marion will still need to address ways to meet needs such as Affiliation, Security, and Religion. In both cases, although they have identified some opportunities that appear able to meet some of their needs, they have not finished their retirement planning. They must seek other opportunities, new opportunities, to "fill in the cracks" that still remain after their initial successful retirement decisions.

Although this process of evaluating opportunities looks difficult, most people are able to work through it without undue hardship. It has the advantage of helping you evaluate possible opportunities and the implications of these oportunities in a manner that ensures you will not be unpleasantly surprised by the implications of decisions you might take.

RETIREMENT EXERCISE 10

It is time for you to work through the process just outlined using your own life circumstances. Do not despair if, like Ted and

Marion, you have difficulty in completing the process beyond Step 8. In the next chapter we will focus on ways to help you do just that. As well, we will focus on other retirement decisions or "what to do now that you know what you have to do!"

Chapter 9

Creating Your Opportunities

"If I had to define life in a word, it would be: Life is creation."
—Claude Bernard, in *Bulletin of New York Academy of Medicine*

For some of you, this chapter will be a waste of time. You are the lucky ones, the ones who are either confronted with—or can create with minimal effort—sufficient opportunities to meet your needs. You are lucky, but you are probably in the minority.

Most of us, whether or not we are considering retirement, are not blessed with an abundance of immediately recognizable opportunities from which we can pick and choose those best able to meet our needs. Sure, we can find some opportunities, sometimes very good ones, but they are never quite enough. There are always some gaps, some holes to plug, if we are to be truly satisfied. It is the skill, the creativity, in filling those gaps that separates those who will have a merely adequate retirement from those whose retirement we all envy.

It is one thing to pretend that the gaps in your needs satisfaction do not or should not exist. It is quite another to pull it off. As much as you try, it is difficult to ignore the nagging feeling that something is missing. And to complicate things further, these discrepancies between what you need and what you have, usually result in a blemish on what you have. Strange creatures we humans!

To create new opportunities requires both hard work and an openness to look beyond the end of your nose, an openness to consider alternatives *before* judging those alternatives as unacceptable or impossible. Because we are dynamic rather than static creatures, we must constantly search for and review our opportunities. Opportunities will change and opportunities that once met your needs will lose their ability to do so. You must go on or go backwards. There is no middle ground.

In the last chapter we looked at a method to help you identify the needs you would need to meet on retirement. The final steps in that process required you to search out new opportunities to meet needs that would be incompletely met if you stopped your search with the situations you are presently considering. In this chapter I will show you how to extend your search by looking at methods that other people have used to meet the twelve needs we have been using as our standard throughout this book. This is not to say that what worked for others will work for you, but learning about it will give you several possible directions for your search.

Openness to the new is the earmark of those who never grow old.

Searching for Opportunities to Meet Your Needs

There are probably a limitless number of opportunities that people have pursued to meet each of the twelve needs referred to throughout this book. Quite often, the action that one person uses to meet one need, another person uses to meet a different need. Needs satisfaction, as has already been pointed out, is a very individualistic affair. With that in mind, I will go through each of the twelve needs to look at how retirement may affect meeting that need and to look at opportunities that others have pursued to satisfy that need.

1. INFLUENCE

Influence is a need that is often adversely affected by the decision to retire from paid work. Typically, retirement comes at a time when an individual has reached the pinnacle of power and authority to be had during the course of a career. And the more such power and authority is enjoyed (and it often is, even though the individual may not admit it), the more of a vacuum there will be to fill when that work opportunity has lapsed.

It is very easy to take the need for Influence for granted in your life, particularly if your work has provided you with many avenues or opportunities to satisfy the need. As well it is common to focus on the more negative side of all that power and responsibility in thinking that you will be glad to be free of the bother of it all. You will be glad—probably for about four months. One need only speak with the spouses of some recent retirees to get a clear picture of how some retirees try to transfer the Influence needs they met at work to their home situations. Spouses—of either sex—make poor substitutes for fawning subordinates!

If you have a strong Influence need, the change that you must make in retirement is in recognizing that influence, power, and authority will no longer be *ascribed to you* on the basis of your position. You must earn it all over again in a new situation and it must also be earned in a different manner. It must be earned on the basis of the persuasion of your ideas, experience, education, or personal forcefulness. Different means, but still very possible.

It is sometimes the case that individuals forget this important distinction and act as if power and authority should still be ascribed to them by virtue of who they are rather than what they have to offer. The pomposity that must sometimes be tolerated in the workaday world is seldom greeted with the same fervor when it does not have to be. Influence needs in nonwork situations must be met in cooperation with other people rather than at their expense. This cooperation means that others must *allow* your need to be met. You cannot successfully demand that they do so.

There are a variety of ways whereby others have been successful in transferring the satisfaction of their needs for Influence from the workplace to the world of retirement. Each method requires a certain degree of risk because, unlike work, power and persuasiveness do not come "with the territory" when you are retired and must therefore be merited.

(a) A common way to fulfill a need for Influence is through service clubs especially since many service clubs are organized on a quasi-military or quasi-business basis with official offices, officers, and the like. As well, most such organizations are organized around a purpose such as fundraising for community events in addition to their obvious social or recreational roles.

Many such clubs welcome the time, commitment, energy, and obvious skills of the recent retiree and would probably be lost without them. If you are not already a member of such a club, maybe it is time to consider joining. If you are a member of one that does not give you what you want, consider changing to one that does. A good point to remember is that although service clubs present a front to the world that their sole purpose is altruism or service to community, they could not exist if they did not, at the same time, meet the needs of their members.

(b) Although you might usually associate service in the voluntary sector as a means to meet needs such as Altruism this is not necessarily the case. Many opportunities such as teaching, pastoral work, counseling, or coaching of others have a strong emphasis on personal persuasiveness. It is not necessary that such service be done "for the good of others" and it is quite possible that by providing such assistance you will be helping yourself more than the person you are supposed to be helping!

Most cities maintain a volunteer center whose job it is to match volunteers with organizations requiring services. Consider short-term volunteering in a diversity of areas. That way you may be able to find something that you are good at—and which meets your needs.

(c) Part-time consulting work, very often in the same field as your previous full-time work, can often assist in meeting Influence needs. Although many consultants joke about the fact that nobody ever listens to them unless they "discover" what has already been decided by the hiring organization, consulting can be a real opportunity for those with special talent. One advantage in doing it mainly as a means to meet your Influence needs rather than as a means to economic survival is that you can afford to be more selective in seeking out assignments that are best for you.

(d) Closely allied to part-time consulting is voluntary consulting to organizations or individuals, even less-developed countries, that need your special expertise. Starting a business, managing people, accounting, and finance, how-to's of every shape and description—all are skills you may have that others may want. Providing such assistance is often an excellent way to meet your needs for Influence. And you thought everybody did these things just to help out other people!

(e) Political activity, either partisan or issue-oriented, is another way to meet Influence needs. Whether it is helping a municipal candidate win an election (or running yourself!) or organizing lobbying efforts on behalf of an issue that affects you, political activity is a natural for the satisfaction of Influence needs. If possible, try to get involved in issues in which you have some degree of expertise or special knowledge—this will maximize the likelihood that your need will be met.

2. Altruism

As I described earlier, Altruism is a frequently misunderstood need because it is one that other people sometimes think we *should* have.

In fact, there are often subtle guilt-inducing cues that other people transmit when our Altruism would be to their benefit. That is not the kind of Altruism that concerns us here since we are more concerned with the feelings of satisfaction that come from aiding others irrespective of whether or not we *should* get these feelings.

Altruism needs are affected less from the loss of paid work, probably because many jobs do not provide a good vehicle for its satisfaction in the first place. This is sometimes true even for those helping professions such as teaching or social work that appear from the outside to be good bets for meeting Altruism needs.

That being said, work is still not a total write-off in meeting Altruism needs and it may be that retirement will leave some gaps in meeting the need that will make it necessary for you to search elsewhere. Fortunately, for the satisfaction of Altruism needs, that is easily found elsewhere in the retirement world.

(a) You have probably observed that several of the tips I gave you for meeting Influence needs could apply equally well to your Altruism needs. It is just that you are looking for something different from the same situation. In fact, most of the situations I mentioned earlier are probably more amenable to meeting Altruism needs than Influence needs even though many people unadmittedly use the situations for the latter. In the case of Altruism you are more likely to get your needs met as a "doer" than an organizer or planner. That is where you are able to get the clearest feedback about the effects of what you are doing. And feedback about the effects of what you are doing is the lifeblood of Altruism.

(b) It is difficult to set out specifically to meet Altruism needs since it is frequently a need that is met in conjunction with meeting other needs. Many recent retirees have found that using their well-developed work skills, this time in assisting other people to do something, is an excellent way to satisfy this need. Thus we see a retired banker coaching budding businesses on the complexities of bank financing, a retired teacher acting as a mentor to teachers-in-training, and a retired construction foreman providing part-time assistance to what he calls "old people" in upgrading their homes.

3. AFFILIATION

Affiliation is a need that many people must reassess on retirement. This is because work is often a major source of needs satisfaction due to the relationships that are often necessary to get the work done. As well, work often provides a focal point for the development and maintenance of these relationships since the work itself is a shared experience and, if nothing else, gives you something in common to complain about!

Most people underestimate the importance of their workplace in meeting their Affiliation needs. Like an old shoe, you do not realize how comfortable these relationships are until they are gone. And, although most people intend to keep up with their important work relationships after they retire, there is usually a decided slackening off, if for no other reason than the loss of a major point of common interest—work.

The satisfaction of Affiliation needs is often complicated on retirement due to factors not directly related to work. Sometimes necessary or desired relocation means that, as well as losing work as a source of needs satisfaction, there will be disruptions in the personal or nonwork area as well. Old friendships may be lost or curtailed; service or volunteer associations may be terminated; important church ties may be unavailable. If these situations are not addressed, it is very easy for the individual to feel quite "lost" or depressed although this may not be manifest until a few months after the novelty of retirement has worn thin.

Successful retirement, as far as meeting Affiliation needs is concerned, consists of building up existing opportunities and developing new opportunities to deal with those opportunities that will necessarily be lost or substantially modified as a result of leaving work. There are few tricks to doing this and in most cases Affiliation needs are met as a side-effect or additional benefit of doing something that meets other needs. It is difficult to establish useful affiliations when the only thing you have in common with other persons is a desire to be with them!

Fortunately, there are a variety of things you can do to deal constructively with the disruption in the opportunities available to meet Affiliation needs brought about by your retirement. As was the case with Altruism, most of the methods identified for Influence are easily adaptable for meeting Affiliation needs and in any case would probably occur as a side-effect of doing so. Here are some other suggestions:

(a) If possible, try not to restrict your search for new social groups to those groups whose target audience is exclusively the retired. Affiliation needs are more likely to be met in a situation where you are in contact with a wide assortment of people. As well, in avoiding such exclusive groups, you are less likely to encounter individuals whose only purpose is socializing. Remember that Affiliation needs are best met as a by-product of *doing something with somebody.*

(b) If you have a hobby that you have pursued solo in the past, consider becoming involved in the more organized side of the avocation. Everything from amateur radio to stamp collecting to quilting has local, regional, and national organizations with many opportunities to pursue useful activity and meet other people in the bargain.

(c) Recreational team or individual sports are often an excellent way to get to know other people in order to form more lasting affiliations. Even for those with minimal skill and marginal proclivity, there is usually one recreational sport or another that will fill the bill—I've had good luck with lawn bowling, a sport I once thought was reserved for the soon-to-be-interred, because of the wide assortment of people it attracts. A colleague took up golf at sixty-five and, as well as meeting a whole new group of people, now cards a better game than I will ever hope for.

(d) A friend of mine claims that if you took all the religion out of the churches most people would hardly notice. While he may overstate the case, if you are of a religious persuasion, don't overlook your church or synagogue as a place to establish or improve your opportunities to meet Affiliation needs. Church can also be a particularly useful source of contacts if you plan to relocate when you retire—even if you are not passionately religious. All churches have secular or business sides that constantly require people and you are usually welcomed with open arms. They can be as good for you as they hope you will be good for them.

(e) Another way for you to meet your Affiliation needs may be by continuing your education. Perhaps there is that degree you never quite finished (or started), perhaps that interest in ancient Greek you have been wanting to satisfy, perhaps that wish to finally learn how to repair your car.

There are two sides to pursuing such training, one being the education itself, the other being the association with like-minded individuals. Either is worthy by itself but you get both as a bonus. Besides, many institutions such as universities, community colleges, and the like offer reduced or gratis tuition for those of retirement age. And forget about not being smart enough. Some of the best students I teach at university are older than I am.

4. COMPETITION

Like Influence and Affiliation, Competition is a need that is often adversely affected by the absence of paid work as a method of seeking satisfaction. While this is obviously more true for some types of jobs than for others, most jobs have a certain degree of competitiveness built into them.

For some of you, that competitiveness may be a chore, something you will be glad to be rid of. Others may find the love of competitive activities "in their blood" whether they admit it or not. For those of you in the latter category it will be necessary to find something else, something from other avenues of your life, to take the place of the satisfaction of your Competition need you were getting from your work.

Remember something I mentioned earlier about Competition. It is one of those needs that you are not "supposed" to have, and most often, meeting the need is done through involvement in activities that have competitiveness as a by-product. For example, an acquaintance is involved in fund raising for a major service club catering to the under-forty male. He loves it but I don't think he is aware of what it is giving him, and in public, he would probably dismiss the activity as some sort of altruistic public service. Altruistic, maybe, but competitive, most decidedly.

It should be evident that many kinds of activities can be undertaken in order to satisfy a need for Competition. This is particularly true if you broaden the definition to include the satisfaction that comes from meeting some internal standard you set for yourself as well as the head-to-head challenge of a footrace. In fact, many of the activities already cited for the resolution of other needs could be applied to Competition as well. Here are some others:

(a) One of the critical elements for the satisfaction of a need for Competition is feedback about how well you are doing. Seek out opportunities where the feedback is short-term if not immediate. Avoid activities where the feedback occurs months or years down the line or is so nebulous that you are never certain about how well you have done. Look for opportunities of a project nature with specific starting and ending points rather than something involving ongoing ill-defined activities.

(b) Activity such as a part-time business of your own can be a fruitful and perhaps even profitable way to satisfy a Competition need. Once again, be prudent in the business you are investigating, remembering that a need for Competition is not a license for recklessness in decision-making. Also, refer to Point (a), above, in selecting an endeavour where the lines are clearly drawn, where your decisions are met by success or failure on a fairly immediate basis.

(c) Sports, be they individual or team sports, are typical means to meet Competition needs. Insofar as meeting Competition needs is concerned, it is usually necessary that you play adequately enough to achieve at least modest success or can demonstrate enough improvement to meet benchmarks you have set for yourself. These are requirements that purely "recreational sports" do not have to meet and may be limitations in some respects.

(d) Very often, doing most anything at the onset can help you to meet a Competition need. Usually, when you start an activity, there is a decided learning curve that is very amenable to the meeting of internal benchmarks for success. This is not always true when you reach a plateau in performance or have lost interest because you no longer feel that the activity is competitive. Learning to use a computer, seeking to understand the philosophy or theology you always found incomprehensible, pursuing a physical fitness regime, or learning to ballroom dance—all can aid in the satisfaction of a Competition need.

In this respect, one thing recent retirees should guard against is a newly found interest and gung-ho participation in the long-standing pursuits of one's mate such as gardening, cooking, or the like. Very often, this participation has a decided, although subtle, competitive overtone and although you may find it helpful in meeting your Competition need it is very likely that it is pursued for altogether different reasons by your mate. Tread softly.

5. INTELLECT

Surprisingly enough, by the time most people are considering retirement, their jobs of long-standing have usually ceased or at least reduced their potential to satisfy Intellect needs. In fact, for most people, this occurs much earlier, usually in their forties or fifties. Many of the very successful managers and technical professionals I see in their late forties, most of whom have jobs that from the outside look very intellectually stimulating, report that they do not find such stimulation in their work.

This is probably because an Intellect need is met only if the task has a certain degree of novelty associated with it. If you have done something over and over again, even something very complex, the intellectual satisfaction of that task is reduced. The thinking process changes from "how to do it?" to "how did I do it before?" Although repetitive work may be satisfying for other reasons, intellectual stimulation is usually not one of them.

That being said, there is still some degree of satisfaction of Intellect needs provided by most jobs, and a minority of jobs can provide a great deal of potential satisfaction right up to retirement.

Individuals with strong Intellect needs should expect that they will have to develop some alternative means to satisfy the need on retirement, particularly since the need may not have been well met even before leaving work.

All of the opportunities that are available to meet Intellect needs share several common characteristics. They are opportunities that will challenge you, opportunities in which you will have no guarantee of success, and ones that will require learning and perseverance on your part. Moreover, such opportunities will be as a late spring snowstorm—potentially powerful but shortlived. If you have such a need in good measure, you will be constantly endeavoring to meet it as each activity in which you are engaged gradually loses its ability to stimulate you intellectually. You will not become bored with learning so much as bored with what you have learned!

This being the case, there are many opportunities available to help you meet Intellect needs on retirement. Several have already been cited for the satisfaction of other needs but there is nothing to say that such activities cannot be useful in meeting Intellect needs. Other activities would include:

(a) It has been said that the present generation of middle-aged adults is the last generation of readers. I hope not but it is certainly the last generation of adults for whom reading was not just the method of choice to acquire new information—it was *the* method. Reading still offers the most diverse information in the cheapest way to the most people and it is a decided method-of-choice for the satisfaction of Intellect needs.

Most public libraries carry a wide assortment of books and periodicals on every topic from how to manufacture your own nuclear weapons to mind-control techniques. In addition, most libraries either sponsor or know about reading clubs or reading interest groups whose purpose it is to stimulate intellectual thought and debate. Most such groups are very heterogeneous in their make-up and may also serve the side-effect of meeting your Affiliation needs. If you can not find such a group, maybe you should start one.

(b) A common method used by men in their forties for whom work has lost much of its ability to meet Intellect needs is the pursuit of an intellectually demanding avocation. Thus we see involvement in hobbies such as amateur radio, computer modeling, precision marksmanship, or hot-air ballooning. There is nothing to restrict such activities to late-forties males and it is common for there to be a good deal of "hobby-hopping" as individuals seek to find new intellectual challenges and opportunities in a variety of fields.

(c) A friend used to meet his Intellect needs (as well as many others I am certain) by becoming involved in the technical side of public hearings on contentious issues such as wilderness preservation or industrial development. Although he usually did not start off knowing a great deal about the technical issues involved in the lobbying, he read voraciously, consulted widely, and was able to put many a so-called expert to shame at the hearing stage by asking questions not usually asked by the general public. Although he had the opportunity to do so, he seldom worked twice on the same type of issue.

(d) Give yourself a Ph.D. I always tell my graduate students that a Ph.D. is a degree in patience and persistence, not any particular content area, and you probably have as much patience and persistence as anyone. Someone akin to my friend cited above, another acquaintance seems to have a different expertise every year. One year it is electronics; another year it is Roman history or muzzle-loading weapons. In each field, he explores, develops, and discards a wealth of information. For him, it is not the content that holds the attraction; rather it is the *process* or *challenge* of obtaining that content.

Yet another friend has been working for years on a diagrammatical three-dimensional representation that is supposed to integrate everything that he has ever learned about management. I still do not understand it and I have heard his two-hour discourse three times in as many years.

(e) A business acquaintance in Canada, formally retired but still with business and family interests that necessitate a good deal of coast-to-coast travel, jokes that his only degree is from "Air Canada College." Of necessity, he usually sits beside someone on his travels, and he uses his flying time to "pick their brains dry" by the time he has landed. He claims that it is like a game for him, trying to get as much information as he can in the little time available.

6. AESTHETICS

Aside from a few isolated fields, Aesthetics is not a need that is typically met through the workplace. As well, my experience indicates that it is a need only infrequently reported as deficient by either workers or recent retirees with whom I have contact. But there are notable exceptions including an engineer whose passion for the design of municipal sewage treatment plants was as much an act of artistry as it was an act of engineering.

For those for whom Aesthetics is an important need, retirement may exert only a very modest need for change in how you are presently meeting the need. Given the minimal opportunities for the satisfaction of this need typically provided by most jobs, it is likely that the satisfaction you are currently obtaining for Aesthetics needs is coming from nonwork situations even before you retire. Unless you contemplate other large scale changes such as relocation on retirement, you may well be able to go on with whatever you are currently doing for satisfaction.

However, you may be an individual for whom retirement will necessitate some changes or diminishing in the opportunities to meet Aesthetics needs. Or, such needs may not have been sufficiently met before retirement and may require attention in any event. Here are some methods that others have successfully used to deal with this issue:

(a) It is likely that, if Aesthetics needs have been important to you through the course of your life, you will have undertaken some type of concrete activity at some point in your life to deal with this need. This may have been some type of artistic endeavour that you pursued and then abandoned many years ago. (I am still storing a selection of photographic darkroom equipment I have not used since I was thirty-three.) This pursuit may have been abandoned for a variety of reasons: lack of time, perceived lack of talent, costs, or whatever.

Unlike Intellect needs where repeated activity becomes diminished in its ability to reduce the need, Aesthetics needs often respond favorably to "repeating the past," and one thing that you might try is to reintroduce yourself to needs satisfiers that you have used in the past. Far from losing their needs satisfying power, they may actually have increased it during an extended "aging period." (Maybe there is yet hope for my decaying photographic enlarger!) As well, your reasons for abandoning such activity—competitiveness, financial gain, or the like—may no longer apply.

(b) Since Aesthetics needs are satisfied by a variety of activities ranging from hiking to music to art appreciation, it is important that you identify *things you will do* that will be meaningful to you—and then do them. Very often such activities can be integrated into things you might be doing to satisfy other needs—killing two birds with a single stone.

(c) Educational activities, particularly in the arts and technologies are often means to the satisfaction of Aesthetics needs. Remember that the criterion for enjoyment is not world-class skills or competence—rather, it is the enjoyment itself.

7. SECURITY

If you refer again to the definition of Security you will see that it is not focused on economic issues although it is possible that such issues could influence your Security needs. Rather, the definition is focused on the psychological security that accompanies predictability and sureness in terms of one's day-to-day existence. Knowing where your next meal is coming from would probably be included but so would more psychological concerns of knowing that you will be able to meet other needs, that you are loved and respected, and so on—anything that contributes to that feeling of well being sometimes referred to as "psychological safety."

To the extent that work is important to you, to the extent that it meets a variety of your needs, and to the extent you feel confident that you will be able to find alternative ways of meeting your needs, your Security will be impacted by leaving paid work. The less your work provides you need satisfiers other than a paycheck, the less impact it will have on your Security when you leave it.

The less your work provides you, the less impact leaving work will have for you.

Security needs are not met directly in many instances and tend to be met as a side-effect in those situations where there is a reasonable expectation that your other needs will be satisfied. As such, you cannot address Security needs in an isolated way when you retire— satisfaction is in terms of your assessment of the security of the "climate" you will enter on retirement.

Interestingly enough, Security is a need that many recent retirees report as being adversely affected by their retirement. This is undoubtedly because it is an excellent barometer of how well they perceive their other needs are being met or, at least, their perception of the probability of meeting their other needs in their current circumstances.

Because Security needs are often satisfied indirectly rather than through concrete activity, it is probably more appropriate to look at a few guidelines to ensure satisfaction than it is to look at specific activities as we have done for the other needs.

(a) Expect that your retirement, like any other large scale event in your life, will have an impact on your Security needs and plan accordingly. The unhappiest retirees I see are those who either expected that nothing would change or those who put their head in the sand, claiming that there was "nothing they could do anyway." Retirement *will* affect you and if Security needs are important to you, the effect may be acute. Depending on the individual, the change on retirement can be similar in scope to the change required after the death of a spouse, a cross-country relocation, or the "empty-nest syndrome." You may try to ignore it but it will not ignore you.

(b) Plan for your retirement well before it actually occurs. It is always easier (and you will be less subjective in doing so) to start your planning process *before* you are swept up in the actual events. If you have done nothing before retirement and are reading this in a panic after the events have swept you up, schedule a break or some "away from home" thinking time to work through the process described in this book. You cannot successfully start off your planning with "what am I going to do now?" That is the end point of retirement planning—not the beginning.

(c) Discuss your retirement with your spouse. This is particularly important in terms of Security needs because often one spouse will look to the other to meet needs that the other spouse is either unable or unwilling to meet. It is seldom fruitful to transfer all of one's Security needs to one other person. Remember that *you* are responsible for meeting your own needs and in doing so will meet your needs for Security.

Retiring from work will change the opportunities for meeting your needs—it will not reduce such opportunities.

8. RECOGNITION

The caricature of the aging manager involves the fawning of subordinates, the deference of freshly scrubbed initiates, or the unspoken escorting to the best table in a favorite lunchtime haunt. Even if none of these perks apply in your case, it is still likely that retirement will impact on the satisfaction of your Recognition needs. This is because work often provides a rich environment in which to undertake activities that satisfy Recognition needs, and many individuals have never looked outside of work in any serious way to meet such needs.

In most cases, it is the structure of working life that provides the opportunity to meet Recognition needs, not that you are doing something so spectacular that everyone will remember you with awe. The hierarchical structure, coupled with the wisdom of "knowing the ropes" that you have accumulated over the years, means that work may be more meaningful to you in meeting your Recognition needs that you realize.

In fact, this is one area that is often noted by recent retirees as a real loss—their recognition no longer comes automatically from the "what do you do?" that is often a leading question asked when meeting someone. If Recognition is an important need for you, and unless you take some concrete steps to replace work as a major source of meeting your Recognition needs, it is quite possible that you may feel that the answer to the "what do you do?" question is "nothing." Worse yet, you may start to feel that you really are "nothing," a feeling that gives rise to the depression observable in some recent retirees.

The need for the recent retiree to find alternative means of meeting this need is similar to the need for at-home parents to find alternative means of meeting the need once their nest is empty. For those who work in paid employment, work provides a common way sanctioned by society to meet Recognition needs in a manner similar to the opportunities child-rearing can provide for at-home parents. But work does not provide the only means to do so—before or after retirement.

Like many of the needs we have already looked at, retirement means that the satisfaction of Recognition needs will no longer occur automatically in your altered lifestyle. It will become something you must pursue rather than take for granted. Once you recognize this necessity, you will probably find that there are many opportunities to do so. Here are some of the more common ones:

(a) Since Recognition is a need that is met by undertaking activities that are both observable and deemed important by others, it is evident that satisfaction will be elusive for the hermit. Meeting the need must occur in the public eye, no matter how small that public is.

Although you may view with relief the fact that you no longer have to associate with co-workers and colleagues on a regular basis, that relief is often short-lived after retirement.

The down-side to the reality of retirement is that although you no longer have to put up with individuals you cannot stand, you are also removed from contact with the work-structure that can also provide for the meeting of your needs, particularly Recognition needs.

If Recognition is important for you, and it is somewhat important for just about everybody, you must involve yourself in some new *structure* to meet that need. And you must *do something* within that structure in order to be recognized. That structure can be a volunteer group, service club, neighborhood, new work situation, political party, or professional association. But, it must be something.

(b) Do not look exclusively to your family or extended family to meet your Recognition needs. It is usually easier to develop new means of meeting the need outside of the family than it is to change the well-established pattern of meeting it that already exists within your family. Besides, there is always the likelihood that recognition given by the family will not be as strong in terms of satisfaction-potential than outside recognition and there is also the tendency to demand recognition within the family (subtly or otherwise) rather than earn it. This usually creates additional stress in a family situation that will already experience enough stress as a result of retirement.

(c) It is possible, if not probable, that you can meet your Recognition needs at the same time as you are meeting other needs such as Influence, Competition, or Intellect. Doing well at activities associated with meeting these other needs may mean that you meet your Recognition need as a side-effect. Refer to suggested activities already cited for other needs to see if some activities can be made to do "double duty." Remember that a Recognition need is met not just by doing an activity but by doing well and by having that "doing well" noted by others.

(d) Look especially to avocational interests you have pursued during your working years to identify possible activities that will help you in meeting Recognition needs. Especially to be considered should be hobbies or aesthetic interests that, while they were originally pursued for other reasons, can be easily reoriented to meet Recognition needs.

On retirement, opportunities to meet Recognition needs will switch from who you are to what you are doing.

9. ADVENTURE

It is the anticipated satisfaction of Adventure needs that forms part of retirement's attraction for many people. This is because, by the time they are contemplating retirement, most workers report that their jobs have lost their ability to meet this need—if this ability was ever present in the past!

Unfortunately, for many retirees, the Adventure need is not well met in retirement, just as it is usually not met throughout their working life. This is due to two factors. They have an overly conservative outlook, and for many retirees, they will be so affected by the loss of opportunities to meet other important needs, that the need for Adventure may assume less relative importance. In addition, individuals may feel that they have to choose between meeting Security or Adventure needs, and since Security may be adversely affected by retirement, they may feel that they cannot risk any more disruption.

Activities that meet Adventure needs may involve a fast pace or be exciting but even these attributes will pale with repetition. Perhaps the most important thing to keep in mind with respect to meeting Adventure needs is that the key word in the definition of the need is *change*. Change is very much a self-defined characteristic and it is also what might be called a "floating point" characteristic, one in which the satisfying power disappears almost as soon as you touch it.

Here are some guidelines to keep in mind in seeking to meet your Adventure needs on retirement:

(a) Many people make the mistake of selecting activities that do not necessarily meet their Adventure need but ones that they can brag about to their friends and acquaintances. They mistake Adventure for Competition, Recognition, or some other such need and choose activities that are not inherently interesting to them but ones that have high marketability on the cocktail and dinner party circuit! There is a simple rule of thumb. If the pictures you took are more important to you than what you did, you are probably satisfying needs other than Adventure!

(b) Since the key word in defining the meeting of Adventure needs is change, don't look to any single activity to do the trick for you. Rather than trying to think of a single activity, think instead of a process or ongoing cluster of activities. For example, don't think that one trip to Europe or South America will satisfy you for long. Such specifics might form part of a "package" but are unlikely to stand on their own.

(c) Adventure needs can often be met by doing what others consider quite ordinary—but they have done such activities already and you have not! Learning to ride a horse may be adventurous for you but is unlikely to meet my Adventure needs as I was born on a farm. Now, where we go once we both know how to ride, that's another question!

(d) One of the reasons that preretirement life may seem adventurous is not so much *what* is being done but the fact that there is considerable variety and a hectic pace in doing it. Bringing about that same variety in your retirement life, as necessary prerequisities to meeting a variety of your needs, will ensure that your Adventure need will be met as a by-product. If you stop, any chance of meeting your Adventure needs stops with you.

(e) Meeting Adventure needs does not have to be expensive. A hiking trip in Tibet might suffice for a while, but so might a program of hiking or climbing within twenty miles of your home. As well, more modest attempts usually mean that your Adventure needs can be met without the usual trade-off that occurs in meeting other needs such as Security.

10. FREEDOM

Even more than Adventure, the satisfaction of Freedom needs is often taken for granted in retirement. After all, the sudden release from all of the personal constraints imposed by working can seem like the first real freedom you have ever experienced. But there is a catch. With such freedom goes the loss of an ability to let others do your deciding for you—and that can be a little frightening.

Part of the difficulty with the Freedom need on retirement is that you may have overestimated its strength. Because there may have been only a few opportunities to meet the need throughout your working life, the need may seem stronger than it really is. (The mechanics and importance of this process have been discussed earlier.) When you are given the opportunity to meet your Freedom need, you may find that your desire to do so has diminished considerably.

In this respect, Freedom is the one need for which it is difficult to identify specific activities that might lead to meeting the need. The resolution of the Freedom need is more of a psychological issue than a physical one—a sense of meeting the need might be accompanied by undertaking a specific activity or no activity at all. Where there is an activity associated with meeting the need, such activity might not be so important in its own right but rather for the fact that undertaking it proves to you that you are free!

This does not mean that, if Freedom is an important need for you, you can just sit back and wait for resolution to occur. Rather, you should try to identify activities, perhaps activities that are designed more to meet other important needs you have, activities that by their undertaking will "prove" to you that you are free from constraints imposed by others. For example, this might include an activity such as furthering your education, that, while it may be pursued to meet your Intellect or Recognition needs, can also contribute to the meeting of your need for Freedom.

My experience with recent retirees, even those who have identified Freedom as an important need, is that they are often overwhelmed by the amount of freedom they have on retirement. Through much of their previous life, they have been subject to constraints imposed by others—family, work, etc.—and have always functioned within a relatively narrow band of decision-making possibilities.

On retirement some individuals find it difficult to choose between the seemingly endless possibilities with which they are confronted. It is the necessity of making decisions, and being solely accountable for the implications of these decisions, that can result in a temporary "freezing" or the avoidance of all decisions. It is frustrating to be more free "in theory" than you have ever been in your life and yet unable to capitalize on that freedom in practice.

If this dilemma confronts you, here are some guidelines to deal with the problem:

(a) Forget about meeting your Freedom needs directly. Instead, focus on activities that meet your other important needs. You may find that by *choosing* such activities you are meeting your need for Freedom as a by-product of such choice.

(b) One of the most common methods used to avoid decision-making is to claim that no decision is possible because no alternative is "just right." Most needs, Freedom included, can only be met by taking the risk to wholeheartedly pursue alternatives that are less than perfect. With a "nothing ventured—nothing lost" mentality comes the unavoidable "nothing gained" result.

(c) Freedom needs are not met in a situation where you are undertaking activities that others might think makes you "free" unless you have *chosen* to undertake these activities. Freedom needs are only met by self-directed behavior.

11. MATERIALISM

Materialism is a need that is very much interrelated with other needs, particularly Recognition, Competition, Security, and Influence. It is not necessary that the "amassing" be money; it may be other artifacts such as old bottles, antiques of all sorts, cars, etc. Keep in mind that the Materialism need is psychological, unrelated to the obvious necessity of needing enough economic resources to keep body and soul together. It is a need that cuts across all economic strata from the individual who has barely enough to maintain a decent standard of living to the individual who could "buy or sell" most of us.

The importance in distinguishing Materialism from other needs is the motivation behind the amassing. In the case of Materialism, the motivation is unto itself whereas in the case of the other needs, the amassing is done in order to impress others, beat others, alter the opinion of others and so on. The stereotype of meeting a Materialism need would be an antique car or button collector who did not tell anyone else what was being collected.

The only change in the opportunities to meet a Materialism need that will result from retirement is the loss of a regular salary or bonuses usually associated with most employment. In some, if not most, cases, this loss will be buffered by a pension or other retirement entitlements. In some instances retirement will result in a larger net income than that available during the working years.

For most individuals, the opportunities to meet Materialism needs expand substantially after retirement. Not that retirement spells "open season" on becoming a millionaire (in money or other commodity) but it can provide you with the time necessary to pursue opportunities that might do just that. Remember that for the person with a strong Materialism need it is not the money (or buttons!) that is important; it is the amassing of same.

Here are some guidelines for the meeting of Materialism needs:

(a) Like most of the needs that I have outlined, Materialism needs are seldom met in isolation from other needs. It is very unlikely that an individual would enjoy amassing money or other things solely for the meeting of Materialism needs and very likely that other needs such as Competition or Recognition would also be involved.

As we have seen, many opportunities can be made to do "double duty" in meeting more than one need at the same time. For example, undertaking part-time consulting after retirement might meet a need for Materialism but might also be important for the meeting of Intellect or Recognition needs.

(b) Don't make the mistake of thinking that this need can only be met by the rich. Money is a useful, and a traditional, way sanctioned by society of meeting a Materialism need, but amassing coconuts might fill the bill for you.

(c) Remember that, as strong as this need might be for you, you have other needs. Do not hamstring yourself by thinking that all of your needs can be met through the amassing of money (or coconuts). The reason that "money can't buy happiness" is that happiness is usually something bigger than the satisfaction of a Materialism need.

12. RELIGION

Like the last three needs described, Religion is a need whose satisfaction will probably be only minimally influenced by retirement. This is because most individuals do not rely heavily on their work to meet this need. It is usually met in the nonwork aspects of their life. Where increased opportunities are brought about by retirement, these will primarily be a result of the increased time available.

In some cases, the Religion need is met indirectly through work, usually as a result of the interpersonal contacts provided in the working situation. That is not to say that most working situations provide you with the opportunity to proselytize in an active fashion but it is usually possible to do something, probably in conjunction with meeting other needs such as Altruism.

The change for recent retirees will be that these unstructured and informal work-related opportunities to meet a Religion need may be reduced. In most cases however, the search for the meeting of other needs in retirement will result in new informal opportunities that will indirectly fill the bill so far as Religion needs are concerned. Other opportunities might include the following:

(a) Most organized religious organizations run on the power of volunteers and new volunteers are always in demand. There are always opportunities available including lay ministering, teaching, fundraising, visiting the sick, or accounting. Remember that many of these types of activities can also be useful in meeting other needs you may have.

(b) A number of recent retirees have met their Religion needs through formal training in religion and theology with an eye to part-time pastoral duties. For some, this has expanded to another full-time career in missionary or domestic service. This is a big step but one that may be worth considering dependent on the strength of your Religion need.

(c) Many opportunities exist for meeting Religion needs through nondenominational voluntary organizations that have a particular moral or religious orientation. Groups dealing with sectors such as the urban poor, abortion issues, rural disintergation, or minority rights often have a diverse religious orientation and are always hungry for assistance.

Examples Revisited

Here are two examples carried forward from the last chapter to help you apply the information in this chapter. The first example is Ted, the owner of a small electrical contracting company. The second is

Marion, the librarian in a municipal library. In each case, we are considering Step 8 from the problem-solving method outlined in the previous chapter.

Ted's Unmet Needs

Here is a review of Step 7 for Ted, his revised list of unmet needs (and the importance of each) after completing Steps 1 through 6.

Influence	Low
Competition	Medium - High
Materialism	Low
Freedom	Low
Recognition	Medium
Aesthetics	Low
Altruism	Low
Affiliation	Medium

RATIONALE

It is evident that, as a minimum, Ted still requires additional activities that will assist him in meeting his Competition, Recognition, and Affiliation needs. After a good deal of soul-searching, Ted had decided that it was possible to meet his Competition and Recognition needs through much the same types of activities since it became evident to him that the most important recognition in his eyes was that received from competing—and winning. As well, since much of the activity associated with meeting these needs must be done in conjunction with others, he reasoned that his Affiliation needs might be met as well if the competitiveness was not at a cut-throat level.

Opportunity

Ted's fraternal organization had recently decided to undertake an ambitious five-year building program that included a recreational center and accommodation for senior citizens. In the main, the structures were being built commercially but there was a management committee that was to oversee all aspects of the building program.

Although he had considered volunteering to chair this committee and take a very active part in the new venture, Ted had previously hesitated to do so. Now, with a good deal more thought, he saw the opportunity not so much in terms of what it would demand of him but rather in terms of what it would give him.

Effects

This opportunity would impact all of Ted's unmet needs (as well as ones such as Altruism that were not particularly strong) but with an emphasis on Recognition. In addition, his Competition need would have a good chance of being met through the give-and-take monitoring that would be necessitated in managing a project of this scale.

Marion's Unmet Needs

Here is a review of Step 7 for Marion, her revised list of unmet needs (and the importance of each) after completing Steps 1 through 6.

Recognition	Low
Influence	Low
Affiliation	Medium - High
Intellect	Low
Security	Medium
Altruism	Low
Religion	Medium
Adventure	Low

RATIONALE

As a minimum, Marion requires activities that will help her to better meet her Affiliation, Security, and Religion needs. Although Marion had decided to take advantage of the opportunity for foreign service detailed in the previous chapter, she was unaware of how accepting this opportunity might impact on other of her demands for satisfaction of her needs. Although she would not actually take up her foreign service for several months, Marion had spent a good deal of effort in researching the area and attempting to find out other opportunities that might interest her in the same locale. Eventually she outlined the following possibility.

Opportunity	Effects
1. Possibility of undertaking additional responsibility as supervisor and counsellor in the women's student residence at the university in the third-world country where she would act as librarian.	Although this was not a perfect solution and one that involved a good deal more work for her, Marion saw this as an excellent temporary "safety valve" in terms of meeting her Affiliation needs. This added assignment, for only one year, would give her breathing room to look for other opportunities on-site.
2. Marion would pursue the possibility of including a theological and religious area of emphasis in the books she would develop in the university library in her new assignment.	While admitting that this was more indirect an approach to meeting her Religion needs than she might have wanted, Marion did see this as a viable alternative in the short run.

Action Is the Key

It should be evident that the opportunities I have cited for the satisfaction of your needs are based on a proactive orientation. Needs are far too important to leave their satisfaction to chance. In fact, the major factor that I can identify in separating those individuals who are satisfied in their retirement from those who are not satisfied is an action orientation. Other things being equal, those who are satisfied *do things*. Those who are not satisfied complain or lament their fate.

A satisfying retirement is not given—it is taken.

Chapter 10

Common
Retirement
Problems

"The common problem, yours, mine, everyone's
Is—not to fancy what were fair in life
Provided it could be—but, finding first
What may be, then how to make it fair
Up to our means."
　—Robert Browning, "Bishop Blougram's Apology"

"But Don't You Ever Get Bored?"

Ask any three retirees for their opinion of the problems that *other* retirees endure and chances are that boredom will top the list. Fact is that you might be able to ask *any* three people this question and find that boredom does pretty well for itself. Not that most people are not busy, but busy or not, they are often bored.

Boredom is a basic human condition but it affects different people in different ways. In some cases, boredom results in almost total inactivity. In other cases, the activity may be as frantic as it is personally unsatisfying. Boredom is not defined by the type or level of activity engaged in but rather by the *meaningfulness* of that activity. Boredom is self-defined.

There are two types of boredom observable in the retired person. The first might be called *acute* and is usually noticed in the first two to six months following retirement, after the initial bloom is off the retirement rose. It comes and goes for the retired individual in much the same way as it comes and goes for everyone else. The second, or *chronic* type of boredom, may also start within the same time frame but carries on seemingly forever, becoming more a way of life than a specific malaise.

Acute boredom is not terminal but it may be damned aggravating. It results from a restriction or change in the opportunities available to meet your needs and usually resolves itself on the basis of finding new need-satisfying opportunities and pursuing them successfully. In fact, acute boredom acts as a healthy motivating force to spur you on to do just that.

Chronic boredom is another matter. It is a state of hopelessness in which you give up on the possibility of ever being satisfied or happy. If you are chronically bored, each new opportunity is either ignored or interpreted as impossible. In such cases, you "define away" any chance of being happy and concentrate instead on ensuring that those around you share a similar fate. Chronic boredom may indeed be life-threatening—for the individual so afflicted and everyone around that individual.

The essential element in distinguishing between the two types of boredom is the perception of personal control. In the first case, acute, you know you are bored because of something you are doing or not doing. You know it is up to you to do something to change your circumstances in order to resolve the problem. In the case of chronic boredom, the boredom is always seen as somebody else's fault. Somebody else has done or not done something that keeps you in your state of perpetual unhappiness. If only *they* would do something differently, you would feel better—or so you tell them.

The theme song for the chronically bored is called, "I am unhappy. What are *you* going to do about it?"

Retirement often intensifies and focuses the feelings of boredom that you have experienced at different times throughout your life. After all, most work situations, even if they are far from satisfying, usually provide you with *something* worthwhile. If nothing else, most work situations provide you with freedom from having to make tough choices about your use of time. Somebody, or the work situation itself, tells you what to do and oft times how to do it. Before you retire you might tell yourself that boredom is a natural by-product of your work. But what can you tell yourself when you no longer have work to blame?

It is this "personal responsibility for me" that separates those who are successful in dealing with the acute boredom we all experience on occasion from the lingering chronic boredom that becomes a generalized way of dealing with the world. To be successful in dealing with boredom, you must believe that you are responsible for being bored as well as responsible for dealing with that boredom.

Greg, sixty, was a senior accountant in a large branch office of a national brokerage firm. The firm operated on a very "lean" staff basis, and as a consequence, all employees were very busy.

It was common for the brokerage firm to offer a very generous early retirement to all managerial employees, and in Greg's case, he was eligible at his current age. With very little thought, and a good deal of relief, he had eagerly accepted the retirement package. "Finally," he thought, "I will be able to have some time to do my own thing."

Within three months of retiring, Greg was feeling uneasy. By six months, he was quite distraught. "There's nothing to do," he lamented. "I am tired of shopping, watching television, and reading. Maybe I was foolish to think about retiring early."

A detailed analysis of Greg's needs indicated that he had been giving short shrift to his needs for a considerable period of time. What had saved him from the consequences of this avoidance were the few personal needs that his work did meet for him together with the time demands of his work that gave him little time to see how poorly he was treating himself.

Over a six-month period, Greg began to identify and participate in a number of activities designed to meet his needs. He began to undertake accounting services on a casual basis for two small businesses operated by his younger friends, planned an educational travel package with his wife, and took up the flute, an instrument he had not played since his early twenties.

"I am still bored," he jokes. "But I am now busier doing it."

Greg's story is a common one. In fact it is much more common than that of the self-actualized, optimistic individual that all of us think the "other person" is. It is the case of an unexamined life that runs adequately well until someone or something changes the unwritten rules by which that life is operating. Then, change, and the unwelcome implications of that change, result in a headlong charge into boredom—or worse.

Unless you recognize the unwanted aspects of change, it can be a very depressing situation. You were not aware of what made you happy before (perhaps not so much happy as less sad) and are unable to identify what can restore that earlier balance, or perhaps improve upon it. You wait for somebody to do something about it. And you may wait a very long time.

The problem in dealing with chronic boredom is not what to do about it. That is the easy part. The problem is in recognizing your boredom and accepting that there are no solutions except your own. Not that you will not be offered solutions and alternatives by well-meaning friends or relatives, but you probably will not listen to them—and if you do, you should not!

The solution to boredom is not activity, per se. It is not sufficient to make idle hands busy again. The solution is meaningful activity—activity that helps you meet your needs. Simply keeping busy, without considering what that activity is giving you, ensures that whatever you are doing will quickly lose its luster. The boredom that comes after engaging in futile and meaningless activity is particularly hopeless. After all, you tried—and failed—and are that much less inclined to try again. Pretty soon, you will be able to tell yourself, "See, nothing works."

One of the difficulties in listening to other people's solutions to your boredom, no matter how well intentioned their suggestions may be, is that they are not walking in your shoes. At worst, you will receive a number of theoretical, "this *should* work" suggestions. At best, you will receive testimonials—"this worked for me." Either case will probably net possible activities, but it is unlikely that the activities will be specifically targeted to meet *your* needs.

In dealing with boredom, start with your needs, not possible activities.

There are no viable shortcuts for dealing with boredom in your retirement. The successful methods are those that have been expounded throughout *Happily Ever After* and involve working *from* who you are *to* what you need *to* what you should do. It is tempting to start at the end (activities) and miss all of the tough slugging at the beginning. Do not be misled. If you attempt to start at the end, you have only a random chance of finding those activities that are right for you. You will still be bored, perhaps more so.

Here are some other guidelines from the chronicles of successful retirees:

1. Expect that you will sometimes be bored. The natural ebb and flow of a relatively unstructured life, where someone does not tell you what to do and how to do it, is cyclical. There are times of intense activity followed by much less activity. Do not fight this process. Instead, look upon the first signs of boredom as your signal to react constructively, to change aspects of your life. Boredom lasts forever only if you believe it will never end.

2. Remember that nearly all activities you undertake to meet your needs will diminish in their need-satisfying power with repeated use. You must be constantly on the lookout for new methods to meet your needs. Remember that, although your needs do not change, both the opportunities available to meet your needs, and the potential for any activity to satisfy you, change constantly.

3. Remember that boredom is fundamentally a *motivator for action*. Boredom becomes a problem only in those situations where you have given up on the possibility of taking effective action. There are *always* alternatives to being bored.
4. Resist the urge to fight boredom by relying on "filler" activities, such as extensive television watching, designed only to take your mind off your boredom. Boredom is alleviated only by undertaking some activity that meets your needs, not by mindless activity designed to help you forget about your needs.

During the course of writing this book, I met many individuals who have dealt effectively with boredom, individuals from all income levels and walks of life. They share a common characteristic. They have chosen to put their energy into dealing with the possibility of boredom rather than into being bored. It is a simplistic distinction but it works.

My Spouse Drives Me Crazy

Darryl, an acquaintance of mine, retired several years ago as manager of the branch office for a national firm of travel agencies. Married for more than thirty years, his wife had never worked outside the home.

Within two months of his retirement I began to run across Darryl "hanging around" a large downtown shopping mall that housed a corporate client I frequently visited. Darryl always seemed glad to run into someone he knew and would sometimes engage me in conversations that were difficult to break away from.

One day my appointment in the mall finished earlier than expected, and once again, I ran into Darryl in the concourse of the shopping mall. There was a look of quiet desperation in his eyes and I knew he wanted to talk. I suggested a coffee and he eagerly accepted.

"You know, this retirement is not all that it is cracked up to be," he volunteered. "Maybe it is fine for some people but the more time I spend at home the more my wife and I squabble. I think we have done more of that in the past three months than in the previous thirty years. She as much as told me to get out of the house in the afternoons so that she could be alone. I think she resents having me around."

Retirement puts stresses on relationships, particularly the intimate and intricate relationships of husbands and wives or other long-term couples. Even very good marriages are often adversely affected by retirement, and with marriages that are borderline before retirement, it can often be the final straw that takes the relationship to the breaking point. It need not be that way but it often is.

By the time most couples have survived their marriage long enough for one of them to reach retirement, they have struck some sort of balance in their relationship. It may not be a particularly good relationship but it is usually one where the unwritten ground rules are well known and function—at least for that couple. It is the old adage that the couple may not be blissfully happy but at least they know how unhappy they are and have learned to live with it.

Retirement for one or both parties in the relationship can change all that. It can make the relationship better or it can make it worse but it will almost invariably make the relationship different. New ground rules will need to be established, tested, and modified, and since such rules are usually developed without the benefit of talking openly about them, it is doubly difficult.

Take the instance where one party in a traditional relationship, usually the husband, retires. Often, the other spouse has not worked outside the home for many years. It is retirement for one person but what is it for the other? For the spouse who is retiring there is the resulting disruption in opportunities to meet personal needs brought about by the change in personal circumstances. For the spouse who has remained at home there is the "invasion" of personal space by an individual who may now demand more of the partner than can be willingly surrendered. This problem is also evident in situations where one spouse in a two-career marriage retires well in advance of the other.

This problem is worst in those situations where the retiring spouse has met most needs through work and where little planning has preceded actual retirement. The floundering that follows such unpreparedness puts a good deal of stress on the marriage relationship, particularly where the retiring spouse now looks to the at-home partner to meet all of the needs that were previously met through work.

To further complicate things, the at-home spouse is probably used to dealing with the other as a *working, productive person,* someone who is relatively confident and secure, whose needs are being met in a productive fashion. For the at-home spouse to now see this mate as someone who has lost a measure of personal stature, as uncertain, and perhaps even "needy," requires a real adjustment.

It is unrealistic to expect that any marriage relationship can provide all of the opportunities that have been lost through loss of work or all of the support that is necessary in making the transition from full-time work to retirement. Trying to make the marriage relationship fulfill such unrealistic expectations will probably result in a crisis in the marriage. The crisis will mean that the marriage will probably meet even less needs of the partners than it met before retirement. Rather than one unhappy person—the retiree—both partners in the marriage will suffer.

Individuals who are successful in their retirement are those who recognize the finite ability of their marriage relationship to meet their needs and who do not put unrealistic expectations on their partner to "make them happy." They are individuals who take responsibility for seeking out and finding new opportunities to meet needs that were formerly met by their work. Changes in expectations within productive marriages—and retirement changes most marriage relationships—are introduced gradually and are mutually acceptable.

It seemed to be good for Darryl to talk to somebody about his retirement problems and it became evident very quickly that he had not anticipated the problems he was now encountering. "I was looking forward to retirement so much that I never thought very much about what I was actually going to *do* when I retired," he said during our extended coffee chat. "I thought I would golf a bit, putter around the house a bit, and beyond that I did not really think very much.

"It turns out I don't like puttering any more than my wife likes me underfoot, but I'm at a loss as to what else to do," he reiterated in a hopeless sort of way.

As a result of our discussion, I was able to direct Darryl to a voluntary group of retired men that had been established in our community. Through their help, he was able to undertake some detailed self-assessment and was eventually able to identify a number of very productive alternatives to his "mall wandering." When I met him in the same shopping mall some months later, he took the offensive. "Don't worry," he said. "I'm just shopping!"

In the situation where both partners in the marriage have worked outside the home and retire at the same time, the problem is perhaps easier. It is often less difficult for both partners to enter a new situation together than when one person has established a regime that the other person must fit into at a later time. Neither party is "invading" the personal domain of the other and both partners are dealing with the same types of changes in their personal lives. In such cases, there is likely to be a good deal more dialogue, and new ground rules that meet the needs of both partners are more easily established.

There are points in common for sole retirement or joint retirement situations within a marriage. In both cases, you must realize the responsibility that you have to arrange your circumstances so that your own needs are met. But because marriage is a joint relationship, you must also ensure that, in meeting your own needs, you are not prejudicing the ability of your partner to be similarily satisfied. Remember that you are not responsible for meeting your partner's needs but neither ought you to be an adversary in terms of your partner doing so.

It is difficult to avoid the effects of an unhappy spouse.

Here are a few guidelines that characterize how successful retirees meet this challenge:

1. In assessing the possible negative side-effects of any opportunity you are considering, do not forget to evaluate the effects on your relationship with your spouse. Do not assume that what is good for the goose is also good for the gander (or vice versa). If in doubt, talk first and act later. In fact, the simplest and best advice provided by successful retirees is to talk to your spouse. And talk, and talk, and talk.
2. If your spouse has retired well in advance of you or has always worked at home, do not expect that your continual presence underfoot will be wholeheartedly appreciated. This is particularly true if you see it as your place to rearrange everything at home to your singular satisfaction or to comment authoritatively on how everything could be improved. Unwilling spouses make poor subordinates.
3. Similarily, do not expect that you can unilaterally redefine relationships that you have with your children, other relatives, or close friends to accommodate your altered circumstances. You may have changed in what you want from them but they may not have changed in what they want of you. People cannot be coerced into meeting your needs without long-range dissatisfaction for all concerned.
4. If possible, seek opportunities that will take you away from your home situation on a frequent and regular basis. Even if absence does not make the heart grow fonder it does reduce the risk of collision. Absence also means that you are more likely to

seek alternative ways of meeting your needs rather than moping unproductively at home. Allow your increased at-home time resulting from retirement to grow rather than erupt.

5. Discuss retirement with your spouse well in advance of actually retiring. If you are already retired and have not already done so, start now. Explore and discuss each other's needs in a way that increases the likelihood that both of you will be at least minimally satisfied. Share with your spouse the detailed personal needs assessment you have completed. If you experience unresolvable problems at this point, seek professional counseling assistance.

6. If you have a reasonably close marriage relationship, seek the counsel of your spouse in acting as a sounding board, both for identifying your needs and for identifying viable activities that meet those needs. If you have been married for a while, it is likely that your spouse knows what makes you tick about as well as you do.

7. Be encouraging of your partner's attempts to undertake new and different needs-satisfying activities. Your partner does not need your permission but probably deserves your support. Remember that having a spouse whose needs are more or less satisfied is in your own best interests.

8. I have said it before but will repeat it because it is so very important. Talk to your spouse!

Retirement can be a very productive and meaningful time for both partners in a relationship if both individuals spend their energies on making the best of their joint future rather than pining for and attempting to relive the past. But being happy in retirement is not an accident nor is it likely to occur for one member of the partnership to the exclusion of the other. More in retirement than at any other time in your life, your individual happiness is inextricably intertwined with that of your mate. That is good news—or at least it should be!

Bon Voyage

For some individuals, there is a desire to relocate immediately after retirement. This may be a matter of necessity, occasioned by economic circumstances or other practical considerations. But for most people, relocation is a matter of choice, not necessity. It is a choice motivated by a desire to be near family or close friends, experience a more temperate climate, return to one's roots, make a clean break from the past, or some other "psychological" consideration.

There is something very compelling about considering a relocation immediately after you retire. It is always exciting to anticipate a move to someplace new and sometimes the comparison of what you currently have to what you *could have* if you relocated makes your present look pretty tame. But how do you know if such a comparison is fair or simply another form of the "grass is greener on the other side" syndrome? After all, you probably know people who have relocated and were very happy—as well as some people who were miserable.

It is probably easier to identify poor reasons for making a decision to relocate than it is to identify good ones. Poor reasons would include basing the relocation solely on practical matters such as climate, moving not so much *to* somewhere as *away* from where you are, or moving simply because friends or relatives have done so. Moving for such reasons is seldom satisfying in the long run unless a good deal of luck is on your side. More often, an ill-considered move simply leaves you unhappier, farther away from where you were!

Aside from obvious practical considerations, the best way to appraise the benefits of relocating after you retire is to assess the impact of such a possibility on your ability to meet your needs. Remember that relocation, like so many of the other alternatives you may consider, is a two-edged sword. It can giveth but it can also taketh away.

The wisdom of relocation can be gauged by improved opportunities to meet your needs.

Because relocation will change and may limit your ability to meet some of your needs, it is a decision that should not be taken lightly. It is also a decision where you should hedge your bets no matter what decision you take. Such hedging might take the form of a temporary relocation for six months or a year in order to "test the waters" without "burning all of your bridges" at home. Or, your decision might take the form of delaying any possible move for a year after you retire in order to test the need-satisfying potential of your current location given your altered circumstances after retirement.

If there is any good advice given by retirees who have "been there" in terms of relocating, it is to be cautious about moving too quickly. Usually, a delay of several months while you thoroughly explore the pros and cons has minimal negative effect whereas an ill-considered quick decision to relocate can be catastrophic. This is not an excuse for avoiding a decision but rather an argument for prudence in any decision that you ultimately take.

If you are married or involved in any other type of couples relationship, the decision to relocate is doubly difficult. Not only must your needs be taken into account but those of your partner as well. What must be guarded against in a couples relationship so far as potential relocation is concerned is each person talking the other into doing something that neither of you really wants to do. If each person thinks, "I am only agreeing to this because of him/her," the potential for long-term disillusionment is high.

When your partner is considering a possible relocation it is not the time to remain silent, hoping that he or she will "pick up on" your unspoken concerns. It is not true that "being in love means never having to say you're sorry"—or worried—or unhappy. Be candid in discussing your fears as well as your hopes in terms of a possible move. In a couples relationship, the decision to relocate, perhaps more than any other decision made about retirement, must be made on the basis of *consensus* rather than bullying or cajoling.

As an avid amateur radio operator, I have the opportunity to talk to other enthusiasts all over the world. Because of my lifestyle, many of these conversations take place from the mobile radio in my car on business trips or on holidays.

On a holiday trip through the Rocky Mountains of Canada several summers ago, I followed a luxurious and very large mobile-home-bus sporting amateur radio license plates. Taking the chance that the driver might be monitoring a standarized hailing frequency, I called and was immediately answered.

Over the next several hours and hundreds of miles my wife and I talked at length with Gus and his wife, Judy, wandering gypsies from southern California. Gus and Judy had owned a successful mid-sized regional trucking firm and had decided to sell out to a national firm five years earlier when both of them were in their mid-fifties.

For the first five years following their retirement, Gus and Judy had traveled full time across all of North America, returning to California only to celebrate Christmas with their children. For the next two years, they had reduced their traveling time to 75 percent, a concession to Gus's health problems.

"We love it. We have met more people in the past five years than in the previous fifty-five. We have good friends all over Canada and the United States and we are never at a loss as to what to do."

We arranged to meet at a picnic spot high in the Rockies and Gus and Judy continued their enthusiastic story while my wife and I admired their home on wheels. Gus had started out as a trucker, gradually moving away from the operating side of the business as his company flourished. But he loved "the road" and thoroughly enjoyed meeting new people, something their retirement lifestyle accommodated with ease. Judy was the planner and navigator, deciding where they would go, how they would get there, and what they would do in each new location. She was also a most gracious and accomplished hostess on the road.

Visiting with Gus and Judy, one very quickly got the sense of two people who were inordinately happy, very much at home with each other and with others.

"We talked a long time before we did this," Gus said. "I knew I would like it but Judy wasn't sure. So we tried it for a three-month experiment and both knew we were hooked. We maintain a small home in California but this is our real home," Judy said with pride, gesturing to their "mobile castle."

Of course, Gus and Judy's lifestyle is not for everyone. But it is an unusual, attractive alternative, indicative of the kinds of choices that are available to you when you free yourself from the conventional and the expected. But, like most alternatives, its viability must be judged in terms of its ability to meet your needs. To be viable, your decisions need not be good for others, but they must be good for you.

Retirement Planning Is Action Planning

Retirement does not have to result in problems that are different in type or degree from the problems you have already faced success-fully throughout your life. In fact from one perspective, freedom of choice, the kinds of problems you encounter will be easier when you retire because you will have one less thing to worry about in making decisions—your work. Of course, the trade-off in having one less thing to worry about is that you will also have one less thing to blame when things go wrong!

Retirement problems develop and fester for the same reasons that other personal problems do so—*lack of a plan* to improve things and *lack of a commitment to action*. I have briefly discussed some strategies to resolve several of the common problem types as reported by recent retirees. Obviously, the range of problems you might have to deal with when you retire is limited only by your imagination but most of these problems are variations of the typical issues already dealt with in this chapter. The resolution strategies I have already outlined are apt to be useful.

In dealing with the variety of problems that you might encounter when you retire, remember that an understanding of your *needs* and what you are *doing* to meet those needs are the two signposts that will lead you to a viable solution. In fact, any solution that does not take your needs *and* your activities into account is no solution at all.

Chapter 11

Conclusion

"If a man will begin with certainties, he shall end in doubts; but if he will be content to begin with doubts he shall end in certainties."

—Francis Bacon, *The Advancement of Learning*

Few people live their lives the way that "experts" tell them they are "supposed" to. This is true in terms of career planning and it is also true in terms of living out your retirement. Retirements are seldom lock-step, well-planned events and it is impossible to write a prescription in advance that will be right for everyone. This is why it is difficult to give anyone lock-step advice about what they should do when they retire—and even more difficult to accept such advice if it is given to you.

The most you should look for in seeking advice about your retirement is help with the *process* you can use to *help you decide* what you are going to do. It is possible to learn a great deal from looking at the process that successfully retired people have used to make their retirement decisions, even though you might find little comfort in the actual decisions they have made. You now have an understanding of that process, a process that finds its roots in the experiences of successful retirees. It is now up to you to apply this process to your own situation.

Perhaps the biggest problem in making retirement decisions is identical to the problem faced when making decisions that affect you in other aspects of your personal life. It is the reality that there is no perfect decision waiting out there for you to discover—no decision that has only pluses going for it. The effect of this problem is that to move beyond the thinking stage, you must be prepared to *proceed wholeheartedly on the basis of uncertainty*. You must seek compromise solutions to problems, not perfect solutions. To do otherwise is to let your decisions happen by not making any decisions.

A successful retirement is one that you control—one where you make decisions that are in your own best interests. It is a retirement where you know what you need and are prepared to organize your circumstances to give you the best shot at getting just that. A successful retirement is not flawless—few things are. It is based on learning from mistakes and the courage of risking again.

Even though it is usually the first question asked of a prospective retiree, remember that the first question you must answer for yourself is not "What will you *do* when you retire?" It is "What will you *need* when you retire?" The experience of many successful retirees is that if you can answer the "need question," the "do question" will take care of itself.

With your needs as your touchstone you have the basis on which to evaluate the range of options available to you—or options you will create—when you retire. You will be able to carve your own path secure in the knowledge that, whatever you do, it will be in your own best interests.

I said in the Introduction that there is a crisis in our nation today, a retirement crisis whose champions consistently flow against the tide of mediocrity. It is my hope that you will be such a champion, that you will shape a retirement that is right for you.

Good luck.

Index